Sports in the Pandemic Era

Sports in the Pandemic Era

Max Donner

Sports in the Pandemic Era

Copyright © Business Expert Press, LLC, 2023.

Cover design by Charlene Kronstedt

Interior design by Exeter Premedia Services Private Ltd., Chennai, India

All rights reserved. No part of this publication may be reproduced, stored in a retrieval system, or transmitted in any form or by any means—electronic, mechanical, photocopy, recording, or any other except for brief quotations, not to exceed 400 words, without the prior permission of the publisher.

First published in 2023 by
Business Expert Press, LLC
222 East 46th Street, New York, NY 10017
www.businessexpertpress.com

ISBN-13: 978-1-63742-448-3 (paperback)
ISBN-13: 978-1-63742-449-0 (e-book)

Business Expert Press Sports and Entertainment Management Collection

First edition: 2023

10 9 8 7 6 5 4 3 2 1

Description

Sports in the Pandemic Era **chronicles the dramatic comeback of sports after the global pandemic forced lockdowns, border closures, and quarantines.**

Following a near total shutdown in the spring of 2020, the sports industry rose to an exceptional challenge with discipline and innovation. This helped health experts understand how the rest of the world could adapt to the crisis.

Sports in the Pandemic Era shares case studies of sports organizations that quickly implemented major changes to respond to pandemic challenges. The text also shows long-term changes that will impact the industry as the world recovers. It concludes with an inspiring look at the achievements of many athletes who overcame adversity and set impressive new records.

Keywords

COVID-19; sport management; pandemic; health care management; crisis management; athletes; Olympics; Paralympics; case studies; sports technology

Contents

Foreword ix
Acknowledgments xiii
Introduction xv

Chapter 1   March Madness 1
Chapter 2   Project Restart 21
Chapter 3   Marathon Race 49
Chapter 4   Health Perspectives 71
Chapter 5   The Sports Economics Challenge 95
Chapter 6   Virtual Reality 119
Chapter 7   Olympic Records 129

Glossary 147
About the Author 149
Index 151

Foreword

The COVID-19 pandemic is a topic most of society had never conceived of three years ago. But it has had the greatest impact on all areas of our lives since then, only comparable with war. I can vividly recall the early days of the evolving situation in China, as I left Beijing on December 19, 2019, following the World Cup Big Air at the new Beijing 2022 Shougang Venue.

We had been meticulously preparing for the official Beijing 2022 Olympic Winter Games men's alpine skiing downhill test event, scheduled for the new Yanqing Venue in February 2020. Our full focus then turned to the Lausanne 2020 Youth Olympic Games in January 2020, during which it became evident that the evolution of the pandemic in China meant it would not be possible to travel there.

Following some delicate negotiations to avoid loss of face for China or cause a panic relating to the Beijing 2022 Games, the scheduled and very high-profile men's downhill event became the first major victim of the pandemic, prior to the avalanche of postponements and outright cancellations which devastated large swathes of competitive sport for the 12 months that followed.

The postponement of the Tokyo 2020 Olympic Games was the highest profile of these. The Games were postponed for one year and then carried out highly successfully from a sporting context but behind closed doors under a strict closed-loop management system. This then had a knock-on effect of multiple postponements for other major World Championships in Olympic sports from 2021 to 2022, with considerable logistical and financial impact. The sense of uncertainty for the athletes played havoc with their careers and emotions, with some unable to maintain their performance level for an additional year. Others tragically missed out after being infected by COVID, thereby preventing them from traveling and competing in potentially their only Olympic Games.

Furthermore, mass participation sport and activity for children and adults with clubs and facilities were closed down for long periods. This had an extremely negative effect on social welfare and the health of the population and society at large. Yet, on the other hand, sport as an activity played a very important role for society at large throughout the pandemic with many people turning to exercise and sport to help them through the effects of being locked down in their own homes for months.

Despite the closure of facilities, people didn't just give up and sit on their couches with initiatives such as daily free YouTube workouts for kids and families. "Physical Education With Joe," featuring a leading fitness influencer, became very important to keep up spirits and keep kids occupied on weekdays throughout the time when schools in the UK were closed. Some newcomers were encouraged to take up exercise. Home fitness equipment sold out, and there were countless creative solutions using household items as weights and balancing apparatus.

Governments realized the positive impact of exercising on the welfare of society, which can save billions on medical care through a healthier population when it is properly integrated into society. Initiatives such as the UNESCO Fit for Life program have taken on new momentum.

Across Europe, the impact of the pandemic across the sport sector is assessed to have resulted in a drop of almost 60 billion euros (£52bn) in GDP and a loss of over a million employees through the compulsory closure of stores, sport clubs and gyms, as well as the cancellation of events.

During pandemic, when when my career took a sudden and unexpected change in direction in October 2020, I joined LinkedIn to reconnect with those who wanted to do so. One of the especially positive consequences has been the number of new connections I made during the pandemic and subsequently, over the next two years, sharing experiences and ideas with them. Max Donner is one of my more recent connections; we share a common passion for sports business and the Olympic Movement. He is a widely published business journalist who has written over 2000 articles in English and German in the last two decades and is the only American author to have achieved a readership of over two million in the German language media.

I was therefore honored to be asked by him to contribute this foreword for his fascinating insight *Sports in the Pandemic Era*. The book comprises seven chapters featuring case studies that give a fascinating insight into different ways in which the pandemic has impacted sport, as well as how sport and companies have reacted.

I completed this foreword after returning from the Lake Placid 2023 World University Games, which finally took place four years since the last edition was staged in 2019, after the initial postponement and then cancellation of Lucerne 2021 due to the COVID-19 pandemic. Thanks to the significant investment of New York State, outstanding venues in Lake Placid and the Adirondacks showcased 1,443 of the best student athletes from 46 countries and 540 universities, competing in 85 medal events across 12 sports, and also hosted a variety of cultural events for 12 days.

Lake Placid 2023 served as a catalyst to completely revitalize the aged sports facilities, as well as to rekindle the community's ambition, confidence, and enthusiasm to organize major sport events. The citizens, and notably the volunteers from 20 countries and 40 U.S. states have been the heart and soul of Lake Placid 2023. All were very friendly, helpful, and genuinely excited to welcome the world. Undoubtedly the reopening after the COVID-19 pandemic has played a role in the pleasure that everyone had from gathering in person again.

I wish you an enlightening read of Max Donner's book Sports in the Pandemic Era.

—Sarah Lewis OBE OLY

Foreword author Sarah Lewis is a former Olympic athlete and served as Secretary General of the leading international winter sports federation, FIS, from 1998 to 2020.

Acknowledgments

As the conclusion of Chapter 2, "Project Restart," explained most of sports business transitioned to virtual meetings quickly and effectively. I and hundreds of others who cover sports business were able to continue our work from the comfort of our homes with minimal inconvenience. Key events—ISPO Munich, FitTech Summit, Global Sports Week, MIT-Sloan Sports Analytics Conference—maintained robust programming. They also developed good contact and interview opportunities for us to follow a rapidly changing environment as sports developed solutions for COVID-19 challenges. The University of Paris—Saclay did the same for academic contacts in sports business.

Once vaccination passes made in-person events possible—albeit smaller and more structured—industry leaders took the opportunity to project optimism about the future and demonstrate how so much of the industry had adapted to the pandemic with innovation. That was on display at the 2022 FIBO sports business exhibition, Paris Salon du Running, and for those of us in the publishing industry, the Frankfurt Book Fair.

I would like to extend special thanks to the U.S. Embassy in Bern, Switzerland, which worked hard to make sure that I could get all the documents I need to keep working in close to record time. The team provided another inspiring example of adapting to the pandemic with new technologies and good old-fashioned hard work.

Introduction

In June 2020, the global COVID-19 pandemic had caused half-a-million deaths, closed borders, suspended large parts of the global economy, and restricted the movements of most people worldwide. Professional sports, which had suspended most activities when the disease spiraled out of control in March, began to find ways to overcome challenges and restart operations. The PGA Tour became one of the first large international sports organizations to relaunch, holding the Charles Schwab Challenge from June 11 to 14 in Texas.

Golf had some advantages that helped to adapt to the global health crisis. It is an outdoor sport which can easily accommodate distancing to lower infection risks. And the PGA Tour had access to medical experts to develop solutions to hold golf tournaments as safely as possible. Another advantage emerged soon afterward and underscored the role that sports and technologies, that the industry stimulates, can play in health care management during and after a world-changing pandemic.

Before the start of the second tournament on the revised PGA calendar, the RBC Heritage in Hilton Head, South Carolina, PGA Tour golfer Nick Whatney was alerted to an unusual jump in his respiratory rate reported by the "Whoop" fitness monitor he used regularly. He had not observed any other symptoms of a COVID-19 infection, but he saw the monitor findings as a reason to get a COVID-19 test. He tested positive for COVID-19, began self-isolation, and avoided further infection risk for the other players and staff on the PGA Tour.

This experience encouraged the PGA Tour to secure a thousand Whoop monitors for players and staff to use and incorporate in early infection avoidance regimens. This became part of a program that worked and enabled the PGA Tour to hold most of the events on its schedule for 2020. It was not easy and involved challenges for golfers and staff who could not cross borders and adapt to events without spectators and the revenues they generate. But innovative technologies and disciplined players built confidence and momentum to move forward and become a role model for many other organizations that faced daunting challenges to resume their operations in a world where a deadly virus dominated decision making.

Sports fought back against the COVID-19 pandemic with inspirational stories of high achievers who would not let a virus stand in the way of their ambitious goals to set world records that were truly inspirational. In May 2021, three determined amateur athletes set awe-inspiring records on the world's highest peak, Mount Everest, just a year after it had been closed to climbers due to the perils of COVID-19. Forty-five-year-old Tsang Yin Hung of Hong Kong set a new women's record for the fastest ascent of Mount Everest of just 25 hours and 50 minutes. Seventy-five-year-old Arthur Muir became the oldest American to complete the ascent of Mount Everest. And 46-year-old Zhang Hong of China became the first blind man from Asia to climb the world's tallest mountain.

Athletes who could not travel to Mount Everest impressed many others who faced travel restrictions with records of their own. Elite cyclists competed in a novel discipline called "Everesting," in which they recreated the grade and distance of cycling to the peak of Mount Everest closer to home. In July 2020, Ronan Mc Laughlin of Ireland completed the course in under 7 hours and five minutes, besting the previous world record by 20 minutes. Three months later, Sean Gardner of the United States completed the ride in under seven minutes, setting another world record. Then, on March 23, 2021, Ronan Mc Laughlin reclaimed the leading position with a new world record time of 6 hours 40 minutes and 54 seconds.

Across sports and across borders, athletes continued to set impressive records that showed how people from all walks of life could adapt and be resilient in the face of the COVID-19 pandemic:

- Dustin Johnson set a new record score of 20 under par at the postponed U.S. Masters in November 2020, surpassing the previous record by two strokes.
- Manchester City set a new record for consecutive wins by a professional football club on February 9, 2021. The 15th consecutive win surpassed the previous record of 14 consecutive wins set by Preston 130 years earlier.

INTRODUCTION   xvii

- In April 2021, Australian Paralympic runners Michael Roeger and Jaryd Clifford both achieved new marathon world records in their respective competition classes.
- Also in April 2021, Li Wenwen of China set new women's heavyweight weightlifting world records of 148 kg in the snatch, 187 kg in clean and jerk, and 335 kg in total.
- American football quarterback Tom Brady of the NFL wrote a new chapter in sports history. His victory in Super Bowl LV on February 7, 2021, brought Brady's total of Super Bowl victories to seven. The 31–9 win against the Kansas City Chiefs also earned Brady his fifth honor as an individual, Super Bowl's Most Valuable Player. That Most Valuable Player (MVP) distinction also made the 43-year-old Brady the first athlete over the age of 40 to become the MVP at the world championship game of a top tier professional league.

The trios of records set by both Li Wenwen and Tom Brady spotlighted a key factor in enabling impressive sports records to be achieved despite the disruption of the most widespread global pandemic in the past century. Advances in sports science have been making it possible for athletes to extend their careers, recover from injuries faster, and accumulate more experience and skills to take their sports talent to the next level. Surviving a global pandemic and adapting to rigorous health and safety protocols challenged sports science in multiple directions. But the scores of new records set in these most challenging circumstances made this contest an impressive victory for sports science.

Sports business managed to set new records, too.

- Downloads of mobile phone fitness apps reached a record 276 million in April 2020.
- The global share price index of the 55 publicly traded sports apparel and footwear companies reached an all-time high in September 2020 and continued its ascent in the fourth quarter of 2020.
- Sales of wearable fitness and athletic performance monitors reached a record high of 445 million units in 2020.

- The Premier League football champions Manchester City reported record revenues of UKL 569.8 million in the 2020–2021 season, despite a 98 percent decline in game day revenues resulting from pandemic prohibitions on spectator attendance.
- Home gym and fitness equipment supplier GivemeFit of Spain achieved record sales and year-to-year sales growth of almost 250 percent.
- Women's football set an all-time attendance record of 91,553 in March 2022 when FC Barcelona played Real Madrid.

But not all the records set by sports business in the COVID-19 pandemic era were a reason to celebrate.

- Major League Baseball estimated the collective losses of its 30 teams in 2020 at a staggering $3 billion.
- The National Football League estimated the collective losses of its 32 teams in 2020–2021 at an even more staggering $4 billion.
- New Zealand's legendary All Blacks rugby franchise reported a record loss of NZ$ 34.6 million (US$ 22.5 million) as quarantines and travel bans decimated sources of revenues.

The perseverance of both athletes and sports organization managers through the worst days of the COVID-19 pandemic has provided both the sports world and the business community with valuable lessons about how to overcome adversity. Try for the best but prepare for the worst.

The impressive success of achieving new records in sports occurred against a backdrop of sacrifice and tragedy. COVID-19 infections ripped through large parts of the sports community where rigorous testing and limits on contacts could not overcome the demands of contact sports and the realities of travel in a world turned upside down by waves of infections, border closures, and local lockdowns. Experience showed that in certain indoor sports, such as wrestling and basketball, eliminating the risk of COVID-19 infections was effectively impossible. And the alternative of discontinuing competition in a particular sport raised the risk of damaging the training infrastructure so much that rebuilding later would be a huge challenge.

As the pandemic wore on, the probability that COVID-19 would persist for the foreseeable future became a new and unpleasant challenge. Health experts began discussing scenarios of endemic infections—worse in some locations than others, with some effective treatments—but not being fully eradicated like smallpox. Frank Ulrich Montgomery, Chairman of the World Medical Association, predicted that COVID-19 would continue to spread for the foreseeable future.

In this context, the importance of somehow maintaining the strengths of sports training infrastructure to help bolster public health became all the more important. A series of studies confirmed that the physically fit were much less likely than the general population to become seriously ill with COVID or die from COVID infections. And the studies underscored the elevated health risks of chronic obesity.

The highest achievers in sports frequently showed that their demanding regimens also put athletes at exceptionally high risk of contracting COVID-19. Golfer Jack Nicklaus, celebrated as the greatest athlete of all time, was one of the first to get—and recover from—COVID-19. Dustin Johnson, ranked in first place as the world's best golfer in 2020, also battled a COVID-19 infection. Top-ranked tennis player Novak Djokovic, five-time FIFA Balon d'Or winner Cristiano Ronaldo and archrival Lionel Messi, World Boxing Champion Tyson Fury, NFL Most Valuable Player Aaron Rodgers, and the NFL's top ranked quarterback, Tom Brady, also contracted COVID infections.

Top-ranked athletes who confronted COVID-19 had distinguished company. The highly infectious disease spread through the community of world leaders and also forced others to isolate in quarantine. The Presidents of the United States, Brazil, Argentina, and France, the Prime Ministers of the United Kingdom, Pakistan, Algeria, and Russia, as well as Queen Elizabeth, Prince Charles, and Prince William of the United Kingdom, and Prince Albert II of Monaco all contracted COVID-19 and then recovered. The Prime Ministers of France and Canada had to isolate in quarantine after their wives tested positive for COVID-19. Frequent travel and hectic schedules made avoiding the highly infectious disease all the more difficult.

The top-ranked athletes who contracted COVID-19 were all multimillionaires who could afford to pause their careers or retire and isolate far away from COVID-19 hotspots. But consistently, they demonstrated perseverance, boldness, and confidence in their determination to pursue high performance. This alone did not make them role models for the other eight billion humans struggling with this global health crisis. But it did offer inspiration to millions of essential workers and many health care professionals who needed to battle the worst of the pandemic on the front lines.

This challenge is not over. COVID-19 has swept from hotspot to hotspot and inundated many regions with waves of infections. Medical research has produced vaccines and treatments that improve the outlook that the disease might have fewer lethal consequences, but the risk of another pandemic caused by another virus will always be with us. Improving our understanding of ways to survive and succeed during the exceptional challenges of a global pandemic will be essential. Learning from the experience of sports will provide valuable knowledge for this goal.

CHAPTER 1

March Madness

Downhill Race

March 1, 2020 earned Tokyo a new distinction in sports history but not the glory that its sports leaders had aspired to. The 14th annual Tokyo Marathon had the potential to show an inspiring preview of Tokyo's latest achievements in preparation for the 2020 Summer Olympic Games. Instead, it became the first mass participation international sports event that had to capitulate to the growing risks of the global spread of COVID-19, a highly contagious virus. As the danger level increased worldwide, Tokyo Marathon organizers restricted the competition to elite runners only and salvaged what they could of this epic race.

In many ways, the Tokyo Marathon was a preview of sports in the first year of the COVID-19 pandemic but that preview was anything but inspiring. Instead, it was a preview that showed years of planning and effort sacrificed to help protect public health, nearly fifty thousand aspiring athletes and their supporters making extraordinary efforts to achieve a goal that was suddenly made impossible, plus hundreds of unrewarding meticulous tasks, such as processing refunds, reversing accreditations, redirecting volunteers, and apologizing to fans and sponsors. Television reached audiences in 117 countries. This managed to cover most of the costs and help the Tokyo Marathon organization survive to plan more marathon races in Tokyo in the future. And, most importantly, top athletes were given an opportunity to demonstrate the perseverance needed to excel, no matter how great the challenge.

Birhanu Legese of Ethiopia won the Tokyo 2020 Men's Marathon in just two minutes and 46 seconds over the previous world record. Lonah Chemtai Salpeter of Israel won the Tokyo 2020 Women's Marathon in less than four minutes over the world record set in the previous year. Both the men's and women's champions surpassed previous records set in Japan. And the event organizers managed to enable elite wheelchair athletes to compete on the course and empower the Paralympic sports movement.

The urgent, difficult, and dramatic changes implemented by Tokyo 2020 Marathon organizers and their health policy colleagues in the Tokyo Metropolitan government reflected the difficult decisions every sports manager would confront in the remainder of March 2020. In just one month, the global COVID-19 pandemic scored a total knockout of the sports industry and left many of the world's strongest athletes down for the count. Good decision making helped by advance preparation made it possible for much of the sports industry to get back on its feet and adapt to the COVID-19 challenge. As businesses worldwide look for ways to adapt to this global health challenge and new challenges in the future, the lessons learned are important for all.

While the spread of the SARS virus epidemic in 2003 managed to be contained by traditional quarantine and contract tracing techniques, COVID-19 moved across borders swiftly and became a global pandemic in the winter of 2020. Even isolated island nations, such as Fiji and New Zealand that were able to severely limit international travel and keep infections at a very low level, had to cancel many international sporting events and limit travel to international sporting events in other countries. For the entire sports industry, "staying the course" and making no changes was impossible.

Large sports organizations and tournaments often depended upon rigorous epidemic control plans to respond to dangerous outbreaks. FIFA's Medical Diploma training program included detailed guidance on infectious disease control. The Toronto metropolitan area experienced an outbreak of the deadly SARS virus in Spring 2003, which was ultimately controlled with conventional contact tracing and isolation practices. Toronto area sports teams intensified their safety practices, but they were able to continue the competition schedule as originally planned and no infections were reported in connection with major league sports events.

The 2003 sports playbook for epidemic control was no match for COVID-19. The World Health Organization (WHO) designated the disease as an international health emergency on January 30, 2020. The WHO then recognized the virus as the highest level of global pandemic on March 11. By March 2020, it was clear that the disease was highly contagious, was easily transmitted by individuals who displayed no symptoms, and resulted in death seven times more often than seasonal flu infections. The annual death toll from seasonal flu typically exceeds 600,000, so the COVID-19 pandemic was on course to cause millions of deaths. Unlike the seasonal flu, there were no vaccines or tested medical treatments to counter the spread of COVID-19.

A closer look at the way the global sports industry was shut down in March 2020 resembles a wipeout in surfing—a powerful wave crashing down on an athlete who loses all control. And, the speed was equally dramatic.

At the start of March 2020, 87,000 confirmed cases of COVID-19 and nearly 3,000 deaths had been reported, mostly in China. On March 1, 167 participants in the UAE cycling tour scheduled to conclude on February 29 were in mandatory quarantine. The last two stages of the competition scheduled for February 28 and 29 had been cancelled following confirmation of COVID-19 infections in two staff members who had experienced symptoms. Further testing found six more cases among the hundreds of cyclists and support staff who had participated in the event.

Columbian cyclist Fernando Gavira, who achieved second place in the fourth stage of the UAE Tour on February 26, became so ill with COVID-19 that he had to be hospitalized for two weeks. Gavira's team, UAE Emirates, followed a voluntary 14-day quarantine. Gavira recovered and regained his strength to notch an impressive victory in the second stage of his first race after he returned to competition in July 2020 and won another stage in a race of the UCI World Tour in August.

While the UCI 2020 Track Cycling Championships in Berlin concluded on schedule March 1, it was downhill from that point. On March 6, UCI announced that three races scheduled in Italy from March 7 to 21 would be postponed until later in 2020. As the spread of COVID-19 closed training facilities and restricted international travel, continuing the racing season with only regional modifications became unfeasible, and on March 16, UCI postponed all races scheduled worldwide until May 2020 at the earliest.

Quickly, the pace of postponements and cancellations began to look like a race of its own. On March 1, the Swiss and South Korean Football leagues postponed their seasons, while five matches in Italy's Series A scheduled for the following weekend were also postponed.

The sports world's attention turned to the Executive Board Meeting of the International Olympic Committee held in Lausanne, Switzerland on March 3 and 4. The media had already begun speculating that postponements and relocations of sports events, which supported the selection of athletes to compete at the Summer Olympics Games, would make postponement of the Summer Olympics unavoidable. As of early March, just over half the athletes expected to compete at the Summer Olympics had secured their designations from the International Federation and National Olympic Committee managers responsible for athlete selection.

The official response reported by IOC President Thomas Bach was "neither the word postponement nor cancellation was mentioned." Unofficially, reports of contingency planning for televised broadcasts of the competitions to be held without spectators began surfacing. As the sports media gathered in Lausanne to report on this developing story, televised sports events with no spectators allowed had already been implemented locally in Switzerland. This was originally billed as a temporary measure.

The COVID-19 threat was very close. The earliest large outbreaks of COVID-19 in Europe, which overwhelmed hospitals and funeral homes, were in Northern Italy, just a few hours' drive from Lausanne. The risk of a rapid spread was high enough that the annual Geneva Automobile Salon scheduled for that week was cancelled by health authorities, although most of the exhibits had already been constructed.

The IOC tried to project confidence that it could adapt to the challenges posed by the COVID-19 health crisis. Bach pointed out that the OBS World Broadcasters Conference scheduled for Beijing on February 24 had been relocated to Madrid and completed its agenda on schedule. He commended the many international Olympic training facilities that had made arrangements for guest facilities to help Chinese athletes who could not train within China during its severe lockdown in February.

Discussion of the financial implications of postponing the Summer Olympics was unavoidable. The IOC reported that it had insurance that would cover the costs of lost broadcast revenues if the Summer Olympics could not take place as planned. While that could prevent an outright catastrophe, it would not resolve many of the other challenges posed by postponing the world's largest event. Securing facilities which had other contracts in place for future dates and enabling athletes to plan their training and travel schedules to optimize their sports performance became daunting challenges.

While rapidly growing concerns about rising COVID-19 infections and deaths in many countries prompted postponement or format changes for major sports events in early March, the Los Angeles Marathon took place as scheduled on Sunday, March 8. Just four days earlier, Los Angeles County had declared a public health emergency after six locally transmitted COVID-19 cases were reported. Twenty-seven thousand runners from across the United States plus 78 foreign countries competed.

Marathon races called attention to the delicate balancing act of sports in the context of public health. Rigorous athletic training has substantial benefits in reducing the risk of chronic diseases, such as diabetes and some cancers. But physical exertion at the level required to win elite competitions creates exceptional stress for the human immune system. Experts estimate that the risk of contracting a respiratory infection following hours of elite competition is six times higher than in inactive pastimes. During a pandemic caused by a highly infectious respiratory disease, extended elite competition poses a risk of turbocharging infection rates if effective protections are not implemented.

Los Angeles Marathon organizers aimed to avoid COVID-19 infections by promoting more rigorous hygiene practices and advising social distancing to keep runners six feet apart. An evaluation by Caroline Delbert published in Popular Mechanics showed that it would require a starting zone nearly four miles long to do this for 27,000 runners. This kind of gap between textbook approaches to epidemic control, which ultimately worked in the case of Toronto in 2003, and global pandemic conditions in 2020 quickly emerged as a major challenge to all sports organizers.

As infection rates increased exponentially and COVID-19 spread rapidly across borders, sports event organizers and sports facility managers were left with only one workable option—a time-out. World Rugby postponed the finals of the Six Nations competition scheduled for March 7. World Athletics postponed the Indoor World Championships scheduled between March 13 and 15 for one year. China's Football Association and Grand Prix organizers announced postponements to dates left open in the future. South Korea's football league and Japan's J-league for football and professional baseball league followed suit. The Italy Cup semifinals were also postponed. Italy's Prime Minister Giuseppe Conte then announced that all sports events scheduled for the next month would be postponed as the country entered a nationwide lockdown on March 9. Images of Italian hospitals filled beyond capacity and dead bodies piled in Italian churches horrified decision makers around the world and prompted them to implement rigorous measures to avoid the collapse of health care systems.

Postponements of sports events due to natural disasters, labor disputes, or temporary border closures have been a recurring challenge in sports for over 100 years. Television schedules planned far in advance have made this more complicated for sports managers to find alternative time slots when facilities and athletes are also available. Increased reliance on broadcast revenues has made this even more important.

Sports organizers rushed to develop contingency plans for COVID-19 related postponements. On March 3, UEFA management set up a working group to coordinate rescheduling of matches by European clubs.

Sports organizations had trained staff to manage postponements. Outright cancellations were another matter. But as COVID-19 related public health restrictions multiplied, cancellations of events that had been planned years in advance became inevitable and expensive. The International Ice Hockey Federation cancelled the 2020 Women's Ice Hockey Championship, originally scheduled for April 2020. On March 9, the management of the ATP World Tour Indian Wells tennis tournament announced cancellation of the event scheduled to start just two days later, on March 11. Of course, most of the players and many spectators had already arrived and had to figure out alternatives for a safe departure.

On March 11, the NBA suspended the 2019–2020 season indefinitely after two players tested positive for COVID-19. A review of the schedule showed the relevance of the term "six degrees of separation" to professional sports. Within the previous two weeks, every active player in the league of 700 athletes had been near another player who had been near the two COVID-19-infected NBA players. Subsequently, eight more NBA players tested positive for COVID-19 infections in the next week.

On March 12, the toll that a single COVID-19 infection could take became more tangible when the entire Real Madrid football club was required to quarantine following a positive test by one player. The news prompted Spain's "La Liga" football governing body to suspend competitions for at least two weeks. Later that day, the PGA abruptly ended the Sawgrass tournament, which had begun that day, and announced postponement of the following three tournaments on the 2020 schedule. That was a quick change from the PGA's previously announced plan to play all four days of the Sawgrass tournament but play the last three days without spectators. The changes signaled a rapidly deteriorating situation.

Major League Baseball's policy change followed quickly and spotlighted the sense of urgency spreading in the sports world. On the morning of March 12, MLB abruptly suspended the spring training game schedule with just a few hours notice, shutting down at 4 p.m. Florida time. MLB also postponed the start of the 2020 season, originally scheduled for March 26.

FIFA joined the ranks of sports organizations adapting to a health crisis on a global scale. It announced the postponement of the Copa America qualifying tournament for the 2022 Men's World Cup, which had been scheduled to start on March 23. Because many of the South American football players were employed by teams in European countries with severe outbreaks at this time, they faced mandatory quarantines of one to two weeks upon returning to South America, and the schedule could not proceed as planned.

The signature sports event for the month of March, the NCAA's "March Madness" tournament, confirmed on March 12 that the entire event would be cancelled and not postponed. The alternative of holding a broadcast-only series of games with no spectators in attendance was evaluated but ultimately found unfeasible, given rising infection rates. In quick succession, the Division 1 conferences in the NCCA announced cancellations of the games still scheduled. Several championship tournaments were already taking place on that day, and the whirlwind of immediate cancellation announcements resembled a tornado.

The financial losses were tough for all U.S. college sports and will take years to recover. The NCAA's annual income from television broadcast rights generated by March Madness tournaments has exceeded one billion dollars and typically accounts for three-quarters of the organization's annual revenues. The NCAA reduced its yearly revenue distribution to the 351 Division 1 teams from $600 million to $225 million. It slashed its operating budget by half and implemented a sweeping furlough program, requiring all employees to take three to eight weeks of unpaid leave.

The "March Madness" cancellation marked a tipping point. Traditional health and safety precautions of the type that Toronto implemented during the 2003 SARS outbreak were no match for COVID-19. And no sports organization had a workable alternative immediately available. In quick succession, the National Basketball Association (NBA), Women's National Basketball Association (WNBA), National Hockey League (NHL), and Major League Soccer (MLS) decided to suspend playing seasons that had already started.

Friday the Thirteenth

On Friday, March 13, the United States Government declared a national health emergency to combat the COVID-19 health crisis. Spain announced that a nationwide lockdown would begin at midnight. France prohibited public gatherings including sports events. The positive momentum that had propelled the sports industry forward for decades reversed course and appeared poised for a wipeout.

Event after event, league after league, and country after country concluded that there was no way to proceed with sports without risking an even more serious public health crisis that hospitals and health care providers could not handle.

- Formula 1 Racing cancelled the Australian Grand Prix, scheduled to start two days later, resulting in a total loss of investments in race and broadcast facilities for the competition and the forfeit of ticket and broadcast revenues.
- UEFA postponed all upcoming UEFA club competitions.
- France's Ligue de Football announced the suspension of professional football.
- Germany's Bundesliga suspended the season after receiving a report of the first Bundesliga player to test positive for the virus, Luca Kilian of Paderborn.

- The management of Great Britain's professional football club associations, the Football Association plus Premier League, EFL, FA Women's Super League, and FA Women's Championship collectively suspended all matches until at least April 3.
- Hungary declared a state of emergency prompting the cancellation of the European Aquatics Championships as well as domestic sports.
- India's governing body for cricket announced postponement of the 2020 season.
- The World Baseball Softball Confederation announced postponement of Olympic qualifying tournaments until an undetermined time in the future.
- The International Ice Hockey Federation cancelled the remaining tournaments of its 2019–2020 season.
- The Augusta National Golf Club announced the postponement of the U.S. Master's Tournament.
- Australia and New Zealand's National Cricket Teams called off the remaining games in their series after the first match was played with no spectators present at the Sydney Cricket Ground.

The avalanche of postponements and cancellations forced sports broadcast executives to make extraordinary adjustments at the same time they needed to transition to remote work alternatives for the health of their own employees. Short-term postponements are unavoidable in sports, and broadcast executives and networks had some suitable programming ready to air. ESPN began airing archived coverage of previous NCAA March Madness games. The Golf Channel began broadcasting select tournaments from the 2018 and 2019 seasons. Extensive data collection and analysis of viewer interests enabled the important business goal of audience retention. Sponsors of previous tournaments received additional visibility at no extra cost. This was far from ideal, but it maintained some revenue streams to keep operations running and better prepared to resume live broadcasts when the sports seasons were able to restart.

Extraordinary measures to combat the global COVID-19 pandemic quickly impacted amateur and recreational sports as well. On March 13,

Nepal cancelled the 2020 climbing season for Mount Everest and its other mountain destinations and suspended issuance of visas for foreign visitors until at least April 30. The closure of Mount Everest symbolized the sudden and chaotic disruption of amateur sports, which had built an industry with global revenues approaching $500 billion a year.

The March 13 closure and attempted quarantine of the ski resorts of Ischgl and St. Anton in Austria highlighted the difficulties of trying to contain a COVID-19 outbreak at venues for mass participation sports. Four Icelandic tourists who had stayed at the resort tested positive for COVID-19 on March 5, but it was not clear if they had been infected at the resort or during travel. An employee of a local bar tested positive for COVID-19 on March 7, and 11 fellow employees reported symptoms. On March 12, the ski resort announced plans to close on March 14 for the rest of the ski season. On Friday the thirteenth, Austria's Chancellor Sebastien Kurz intervened personally and announced a quarantine of the entire area.

Subsequent developments showed that there was almost no effective way to contain the spread of COVID-19 in this type of outbreak. Foreign tourists were not required to shelter in place, and there were not enough emergency facilities to accommodate this. The sudden mass exodus in crammed vehicles enabled further spread of the virus. Ultimately, visitors from a total of 45 countries were found to have tested positive for COVID-19 after their stay in Ischgl. The number of COVID-19 cases traced back to the resort was at least 2,400. Because about 80 percent of COVID-19 cases are asymptomatic or show only mild flu-like symptoms, no one knows for sure how early the outbreak started and how widely it spread.

The scale of the COVID-19 outbreaks which originated in Ischgl called attention to the "Superspreader" risk in sports. Bringing together thousands of people from many different locations, frequent mingling with strangers, and then traveling to different locations exponentially increased the risk of rapid spread of an infectious disease from the sports area. Other places, such as large air transport hubs and cruise ships, posed similar challenges. Once COVID-19 became a global pandemic and the death toll mounted, hitting the pause button on Superspreader activities appeared essential to avoid catastrophe.

Down, but not Out

The global spread of COVID-19 soon left no safe havens for sports. Players from China's professional football clubs had initially moved their training operations to foreign locations in Spain and Dubai. But weeks later, these had to close as local cases emerged.

International borders closed in quick succession. On March 15, Argentina closed its borders to nonresidents. The next day, Canada limited international arrivals to citizens and residents. Brazil banned all foreigners except legal residents from entering until April 30. On March 19, Australia and New Zealand closed their borders to all travelers except citizens and legal residents. Those who were permitted to enter were obligated to complete a strict 14-day quarantine.

In mid-March, the 26 European countries that had permitted unrestricted travel across borders since 1995 reintroduced border controls and banned entry from outside the region. Health care and international shipping workers were exempted, but international sports professionals were not.

Some border closures were even more rigorous. Aruba, Cameroon, Ecuador, Madagascar, and Bermuda closed their borders to all arrivals, including legal residents. Columbia, Peru, and Honduras closed all borders. Kazakhstan and Uzbekistan closed their borders and prohibited their citizens from traveling outside the country. China closed its borders to foreigners, including those with visas and residence permits, on March 28. This made it impossible for international athletes and coaches to organize local training and test events for the Beijing 2022 Winter Olympics or for China to hold international sports events, such as the Asian Beach Games planned for Hainan Island.

Russia, scheduled to host over a dozen international sports events in 2020, was one of the last countries to close its borders to foreign travel. It made the announcement on March 30.

The suspension of access to sports training facilities was also extensive. Decisions made by different national and regional health authorities made this a complex and changing patchwork of mandatory regulations and voluntary guidelines. Australia's "zero-COVID" strategy made it possible for gyms, recreational sports facilities, and elite sports training centers to continue operations except during brief local lockdowns. At the opposite end of the spectrum, hard lockdowns in Italy and Spain kept residents confined to their homes except for essential purchases of food and medical services.

Most countries and regional health authorities accommodated some outdoor exercise choices with severe restrictions designed to prevent the risk of COVID-19 infection risks. England, France, and Ireland allowed limited outdoor exercise by individuals within a short distance of home. Germany permitted outdoor exercise by individuals and members of the same household. Cuba closed gyms, swimming pools, and beaches for two months, but it arranged for elite training facilities to operate with enhanced hygiene measures. Finland arranged for athletes to continue training individually outdoors with remote coaching using performance measurement devices and communications links. South Korea managed to contain outbreaks with sophisticated tracking technology and allowed gyms and sports training facilities to remain open with enhanced safety measures.

COVID-19 showed exceptionally high infection and fatality rates in many communal residential buildings. This posed a particular dilemma for managers of specialized sports training facilities. COVID-19 infections tore through some communal facilities at prisons and nursing homes, infecting over half of the residents. But some college campuses were able to adapt dormitory facilities with strict distancing and hygiene protocols designed to prevent outbreaks. The University of Florida, for example, implemented a program called "UF Health Screen, Test & Protect" while combining in-person and online education. But the IMG Academy of Sports, an elite sports training facility also located in Florida, did not have the scale to implement this kind of plan, although it was the largest specialized sports training facility in the region.

The financial burden of closing high-performance training facilities for athletes and professional teams was high and unsustainable. At an average cost of $10,000 per month per athlete, the monthly outlays for a large professional team which also supports a minor league team to develop future talent exceed $1.5 million. That is modest compared to the payroll commitments of top teams.

The normal expenditures for athlete salaries at the Bayern Munich Football Club had been over 15 million euros (about US$ 18 million). The Los Angeles Dodgers' monthly athlete payroll exceeded $22 million. Covering essential expenses while absorbing large losses to revenues from ticket sales and television rights was a huge challenge for the largest teams with stronger financial reserves. For smaller professional teams and sports federations, the prospect of going out of business loomed large. After the German Bundesliga suspended the 2019–2020 season, the German Press Agency (DPA) reported that German first league clubs risked losing approximately 750 million euros (about US$ 900 million). The report anticipated that the teams with the weakest finances might not be able to survive, throwing the match schedule into chaos.

Clubs and leagues made several quick adjustments to preserve the shared infrastructure they depended upon to produce quality competitions. The clubs in the English Premier League set up a fund to subsidize and support the smaller clubs in the lower divisions organized by the English Football league. The initial grant was nearly US$ 60 million. This was later augmented by a contribution of US$ 330 million.

Germany launched a similar private initiative. The four top ranked teams in the Bundesliga—Bayern Munich, Borussia Dortmund, Red Bull Leipzig, and Bayer Leverkusen—established a fund of 20 million euros to support other teams in the first and second divisions that did not have enough financial reserves to pay salaries when competition was suspended.

Individual clubs and sports federations also took the initiative to reduce compensation for higher earners to support the masses of modestly paid workers whose efforts had been essential to sports event operations. Germany's Borussia Dortmund football club agreed to reduce player salaries by 10 percent for games played with no spectators and by 20 percent for weeks in which play was suspended to provide funds for day workers. Bayern Munich, Schalke 04, FC Cologne, and other clubs followed this example. FC Barcelona in Spain made a much more dramatic adjustment as its players agreed to defer 70 percent of their salaries to preserve the jobs and incomes of the rest of the club's employees. In the United States, Major League Baseball announced a commitment by each of the league's 30 teams to contribute $1 million each for financial support to ballpark workers who had become temporarily unemployed because of the postponement of the 2020 season.

An Avalanche of Postponements

Late March is notorious for avalanches at winter sports resorts, but in 2020, these were overshadowed by an avalanche of postponements that gave broadcasters and sports managers complex and expensive rescheduling challenges.

- UEFA announced that the Euro 2020 competition would be postponed by one year to 2021.
- UEFA also cancelled the 2020 finals of the UEFA Champions League, Women's Champions League, and the Europa League.
- The FIFA Copa America was also postponed by one year to 2021.
- The FIFA Africa Cup qualifying tournament for the 2022 World Cup was postponed indefinitely.
- The Kentucky Derby was postponed from May 2020 to September.
- The Roland Garros Grand Slam tennis tournament was postponed from late May 2020 to late September.
- UCI postponed the stages of the Giro d'Italia planned for May 2020 to 2022.
- The ATP Tennis World Tour announced suspension of scheduled events through June 7.
- The FIA Grand Prix races scheduled for the Netherlands, Spain, and Monaco in May were postponed.
- The Australian Football League postponed the season for men's competitions until June and cancelled the women's 2020 season.
- The athletics Diamond League postponed competitions scheduled for China, Qatar, Stockholm, Naples, and Rabat.

- The 2020 Men's Ice Hockey World Championship scheduled for May was cancelled outright, rather than postponed, given the limited availability of players for future national team events.
- The 2020 Wimbledon tennis tournament was cancelled outright while plans to resume the traditional event in 2021 were announced.

As borders closed, sports training facilities suspended operations, and most international sports competitions were postponed or cancelled, pressure grew for the organizers of the 2020 Summer Olympic and Paralympic Games to announce an effective alternative plan. Many postponements of events that influenced selection for Olympic teams and the uncertainty of the timing for rescheduling them made it unfeasible to implement the original plans for both events. And, border closures that went so far as to deny entry to a country's own citizens made the logistical challenge of getting athletes and support staff in and out of Tokyo unmanageable.

Tokyo 2020 organizers had to make significant changes to the plans for the Olympic torch lighting ceremony and relay, which began as originally scheduled in Olympia on March 12. No spectators were allowed at Olympia or as the torch proceeded on its route to Athens to be transported by air to Tokyo.

Athletes began voicing concerns that made re-evaluation of a postponement imperative. Hayley Wickenheiser, a member of the IOC Athletes' Commission, shared the perspective of working in a Toronto emergency room while she was completing her medical training. In a Twitter post on March 17, she asserted that the COVID-19 crisis was now bigger than the Olympics. She highlighted some of the toughest challenges—athletes who cannot train, spectators who cannot travel, and sponsors who cannot adapt their communications to this kind of crisis. Then Katerina Stefandi of the World Athletes Commission observed that the global health crisis was rapidly deteriorating.

The external pressure that the International Olympic Committee and International Paralympic Committee faced to make a schedule change was much greater than for professional sports leagues that were controlled by team owners. National sports federations responsible for preparing athletes to compete at the Olympics began calling for a postponement, led by UK Athletics and USA Track and Field. Then the National Olympic Committees in Canada and Australia announced that they would withdraw from Tokyo 2020 if the Games took place in July 2020 as originally planned, announcements that were unprecedented.

The Japanese government needed to consider its own COVID-19 prevention measures to evaluate the country's capacity to host an international sporting event and screen international visitors during a global pandemic. Japan's borders had remained open and reported COVID-19 infections were low, but the actual scale of the pandemic within Japan was uncertain because facilities for testing asymptomatic cases were limited. The Japanese government had provided financial guarantees for much of the program and would have to find ways to cover the budget shortfall if the Games did not take place as planned.

On March 24, IOC President Thomas Bach and Japan's President Shinzo Abe issued a joint statement following a conference call that the Games would be postponed until 2021 in light of the global health crisis. The wave of postponements continued, compelling World Athletics, the World Aquatics Federation (FINA), and other sports federations to delay world championships that had been scheduled for 2021 to 2022.

A month so terrible that "March Madness" now looked like an understatement ended with an early sign of hope for a better future. On March 31, VISA announced that it would automatically extend its financial contributions to the 96 athletes it sponsored in the Team VISA athlete funding program. The encouragement started to build positive momentum for a team effort to maintain sports talent so that the industry could restart when it was possible once again.

A Case in Point: German Bundesliga

The initial response of the German Football Association (Bundesliga) regarding COVID-19 infection risks was to leave decisions on playing matches and having fans in the stadiums to local health authorities. Shortly afterward, on March 8, 2020, Germany's Health Minister

Jens Spahn advocated cancelling more large events, including football matches. Bundesliga leaders met the following day and decided to proceed with scheduled matches unless local health authorities decided to restrict them. The first restriction was announced for the first international match on the schedule, a Champions League match between Paris Saint-Germain and Borussia Dortmund. It was scheduled for March 11 in Paris, where local health authorities directed the match to be played without spectators. Then a local match between German clubs Mönchengladbach and Cologne was directed to play without spectators on March 10. At the same time, Italy suspended professional sports, including Serie A football, indefinitely.

By March 13, the COVID-19 infection risks had become so serious that Bundesliga leaders decided on their own to suspend the season immediately until April at the earliest. The executive committee announced its determination to finish the nine matches remaining for the season, but exactly how they could do that was uncertain. The estimate of how much money they would lose if the league cancelled the season was certain, and it was a large figure—over $800 million. The clubs in the first and second tiers of the Bundesliga collectively employed over 56,000 workers. Earning enough to keep the workers' skills available would be important for future success. Borussia Mönchengladbach players proceeded with a temporary solution and agreed to contribute €1 million from their own salaries to support rank-and-file staff. Borussia Dresden, Werder Bremen, Bayern Munich, and Karlsruhe SC followed and encouraged the other teams in the league to do the same. FC Schalke and FC Cologne joined the effort.

Germany introduced a five-week "limited lockdown" starting the next week. Essential workers in health care and utilities continued to go to work, and essential businesses selling food and medicine remained open, but all others were directed to stay at home. Gyms and sports facilities, including golf clubs and tennis courts, were closed. There were no restrictions on outdoor exercise by individuals.

Bayern Munich responded to lockdown restrictions by introducing "cyber workouts." Players trained together from their homes using tablets that let them view coaches and other players. Other clubs followed.

Eintracht Frankfurt's coaching staff shared the fundamentals of online coaching in a training program. It emphasized monitoring players remotely with connected electronic measurement devices and interactive communications to keep players focused and motivated.

A virtual competition was organized quickly to enable teams to maintain contact with fans and broadcast partners. The "Bundesliga Home Challenge" used the EA FIFA 20 game with PlayStation consoles and broadcast the competitions to over 2 million viewers. The first series took place the last weekend in March and was followed by two more broadcasts in April.

After the suspension of the season was extended to the end of April at the earliest, the four leading teams, Bayern Munich, Borussia Dortmund, RB Leipzig, and Bayer Leverkusen, announced a $22 million solidarity fund to help the other Bundesliga and Bundesliga 2 clubs continue paying salaries to rank and file staff. They had already witnessed MSK Zilina, the top ranked football club in Slovakia, file for bankruptcy. This highlighted the risks that the Bundeliga competition schedule would descend into chaos if financially weaker clubs went bankrupt because of pandemic disruption.

While Bundesliga executives were working from home, they continued with the league's largest investment project ever—the construction of a new administrative headquarters and training center for athletes, coaches, and officials. The new building cost €150 million, about $165 million. Construction proceeded and the campus opened in March 2022, four months ahead of schedule. The complex can accommodate events with up to 1,500 participants, a sign the league expects capacity limits of the pandemic era to be temporary.

After the decision to resume the 2019-20 season on May 16 was finalized, the league crafted policies focused on keeping participants healthy and keeping COVID-19 infections at a minimum. COVID-19 testing would be mandatory for everyone in the stadium. A maximum of 213 people would be allowed on site, including players, replacements, coaches, medical teams, officials, and media. Two-week quarantine periods were required for all who tested positive and their close contacts. This policy was put to the test when two players of the Dresden Dynamo team tested positive, and the entire team had to isolate for two weeks.

The decision to hold all matches without spectators was firm. Players accustomed to the motivation and energy of fans in the stands missed this aspect, but they appreciated how much fans at home with few opportunities to watch live sports on television would welcome their return. As Bundesliga CEO Christian Seifert described the conclusion of the season, "It's not the Bundesliga that we wanted, but it was the only Bundesliga that was possible."

When the International Olympic Committee met on March 3 and 4, 2020 in Lausanne, Switzerland, the press briefing introduced social distancing, but the atmosphere was "Keep calm and carry on." By the end of March, IOC decision makers had to conclude that holding the Summer Olympics in 2020 as originally planned would not be possible. The event was ultimately postponed for one year.

Photo by Max Donner, Lausanne, Switzerland, March 4, 2020.

Key Sources and References

BBC.com staff. September 23, 2020. "Ischgl: Austria Sued Over Tyrol Ski Resort's Covid-19 Outbreak." *BBC.com*. www.bbc.com/news/world-europe-54256463.

Berkeley, G. December 23, 2020. "China to no Longer Hold Olympic Qualifier as UWW Reshuffles Wrestling Events." *Insidethegames.biz*. www.insidethegames.biz/articles/1102347/uww-wrestling-olympic-qualifiers-moved.

Bonesteel, M. March 13, 2020. "Further Postponements and Cancellations Leave Sports Calendar All but Empty." *The Washington Post*.

Cyclingnews staff. March 2020. "Coronavirus and Cycling: A Timeline of the Pandemic's Effect on the Sport." *Cyclingnews.com*. www.cyclingnews.com/features/coronavirus-and-cycling-a-timeline-of-the-pandemics-effect-on-the-sport/.

Deutsche Welle Staff. March 31, 2020. "Coronavirus and Sports: What Happened in March 2020?" *DW.com*. www.dw.com/en/coronavirus-and-sports-what-happened-in-march-2020/a-53229343.

Leitch, W. March 16, 2020. "NBA Season Suspended Over Coronavirus Fears." *NBC.com*. www.nbcnews.com/think/opinion/nba-season-suspended-over-coronavirus-fears-our-sports-blackout-may-ncna1160061.

Mackay, D. February 2, 2021. "March Madness Cancellation Cost NCAA $800 Million in Lost Revenue." *Insidethegames.biz*. www.insidethegames.biz/articles/1103746/ncaa-suffer-big-loss-after-cancellation.

Sheinin, D. March 14, 2020. "The Week the Coronavirus Ground the Sports World to a Halt." *The Washington Post*.

Spillner, M. July 31, 2021. "Bauleiter des Neuen DFB-Campus Stellt das 150 Millionen Euro Teure Frankfurter Großprojekt vor." *Frankfurter Neue Presse*.

Wacker, B. March 12, 2020. "Players 2020: PGA Tour Cancels Players Championship, Next Three Tournaments." *Golf Digest*. www.golfdigest.com/story/players-2020-pga-tour-cancels-players-championship-next-three-tournaments.

CHAPTER 2

Project Restart

The Race to Restart

The top tier of professional baseball in South Korea earned the distinction of becoming the first prominent sports league to restart its schedule and adapt to the global health crisis. The Korean Baseball Organization opened preseason competitions for the top ten professional teams on April 21 to prepare for the start of a regular season on May 5. That historic date was 38 days later than the originally scheduled opening day of March 28. Both the pre-season games and initial regular season games were presented as broadcast events with no spectators in attendance. The announced goal was to play the 144 games of the regular season in its entirety. To accommodate the unavoidable delay in starting the season, the traditional All-Star Game was cut from the schedule and the playoff schedule was shortened.

The planned "regular season" had to adopt many exceptional practices and prepare for changes from the COVID-19 crisis. Players were required to use smartphone health tracking monitors, which would alert managers if any had been near a COVID-19 infected individual or showed potential symptoms of an infection themselves. Participants were encouraged to wear face masks when they were not on the baseball diamond. And the league announced its readiness to postpone or cancel games as necessary to respond to changes in the public health environment.

South Korea's ability to manage public health risks during a pandemic was exceptional and few sports organizations in other countries could simply follow its policies with minor adjustments. Traditional track-and-trace epidemic control systems similar to those that worked in Toronto during the 2003 SARS outbreak generally worked in South Korea, with the additional advantage that smartphone usage was universal and helped to make tracking and tracing relatively inexpensive and reliable.

Germany's network of testing centers and universal health care coverage had made it possible to contain the spread of COVID-19 by closing borders, limiting travel, and prohibiting large gatherings. That also made it possible for the national horse racing association, Deutsche Gallop, to resume the racing season just two months after it had been suspended on March 9. On May 7, the season restarted with a full 12 race schedule in Hannover, followed by another 12 races the following day in Cologne. The races employed strict hygiene and social distancing guidelines coordinated with local health agencies and could not admit spectators.

The business model of horse racing, largely supported by online betting, broadcast revenues and sponsorship, could cover the expenses of maintaining racecourses, stables, and management offices, and be adapted to pandemic restrictions. Deutsche Gallop jockeys and field staff maintained their incomes, so that the brief shutdown did not result in any lasting damage to the sport's ability to grow in the future. The quick restart of Deutsche Gallop also provided a morale boost to essential workers who had to find practical solutions to keep working through the pandemic. It was also a welcome opportunity for broadcasters to be able to show live sports.

The UFC Mixed Martial Arts franchise positioned itself to be the first large international sports organization to restart after COVID-19 forced suspension of Spring 2020 sports schedules. UFC events did not require large support staffs to put on and broadcast the fights, which were held in compact facilities. Unlike many sports organizations with a local fan base, UFC was not reliant on ticket sales to cover costs. Cable pay-per-view fees were UFC's primary source of revenue and the unusual combination of audiences required to stay at home during lockdowns and the postponement of other live sports events helped increase pay-per-view revenue potential for UFC.

The challenge for UFC to find a suitable location and get the athletes plus a core team of support personnel and television crews to that location was substantial. Florida announced on April 30 that it would start the first phase of reopening on May 4 and UFC responded quickly by organizing three UFC fight series in Jacksonville starting on May 9. Theaters and arenas remained closed during this phase and large gatherings were also prohibited. Accordingly, the first three restart events were held without spectators and produced no ticket revenues, a policy often referred to as "behind closed doors." UFC continued this policy throughout 2020.

Nevada planned a phase 2 reopening including pools, gyms, and some recreation facilities, but not large events, starting May 29. This made it possible for UFC to schedule five more event series in Las Vegas. The city was also the location of its headquarters, as well as a custom-built training facility, the UFC Performance Institute.

The UFC restart plan employed extensive testing to identify any prospective participants who might have been infected with COVID-19 before they had contact with other participants. UFC administered 2,500 tests for the five series held in Las Vegas from May 30 to June 27. There were no secondary infections from contact with a prospective participant who had been screened out because of a positive test.

UFC found another solution to maintain momentum in the international sphere. The pandemic caused severe travel restrictions for entry to the United States to be implemented in March 2020. UFC management sought an international venue where it could isolate athletes and staff from the risk of COVID-19 infections and hold fights between international contenders. It arranged for a biosecure bubble to be set up on Yas Island near Abu Dhabi in the United Arab Emirates and branded the facility "Fight Island."

The procedure for getting contenders and staff to UFC Fight Island with minimal risk of COVID-19 infections was rigorous and expensive. UFC operated charter flights from four regional hubs to Abu Dhabi. The hubs were Las Vegas, Sao Paolo, London, and Moscow. Participants had to travel to one of the four hubs, test negative for COVID-19, and then quarantine before boarding their charter flight. They were then tested again upon arrival and required to stay within the biosecure facility on Yas Island. This was expensive and time-consuming, but it worked.

The UFC restart events achieved the key goal of maintaining broadcast revenues and the UFC television audience. It also distinguished UFC's professional management credentials and attracted media attention. This enabled UFC to substantially grow its television audience during the May to August 2020 restart period. According to Nielson Ratings, UFC was the only major sports franchise to record television audience growth during the period. The growth continued across social media channels. In 2020, UFC's total follower count increased 75 percent on Facebook, to 53.1 million. The Instagram count increased by 31.2 percent to 24.2 million.

The 10.7 million subscribers on the UFC YouTube Channel marked a 25.6 percent increase.

As sports organizations prepared their restart plans, they faced many policy decisions beyond the demands of a regular season:

- Policies to implement if a player or staff member tested positive for coronavirus
- How to modify support services offered to players to minimize infection risks
- How to manage the training of different players with various local lockdown restrictions that change from area to area and from week to week
- How to schedule and prepare reserve players to step in for players who were required to quarantine or were unable to travel outside a specific area
- How to compensate spectators who had purchased tickets for events that were postponed or cancelled
- Obtaining official permission from local health department officials for all planned activities
- Evaluating insurance policies and identifying exemptions from coverage that require specific policy decisions
- Monitoring changes in visa policy and visa validity so that players and staff of other nationalities can be activated or substituted
- Keeping sponsors informed of changes and timing so that they can modify marketing campaigns and reschedule staff as necessary
- Maintaining relationships with fans, season ticket holders and VIP supporter groups
- Working with broadcast partners to find suitable replacements for cancelled events and monitoring broadcast schedule changes across the industry to achieve the best audience potential and brand recognition
- Create and update content for channels on YouTube and other media directly managed by the sports organization

- Modify contracts affected by changes resulting from pandemic restrictions and safety precautions
- Adjust formulas used to determine performance rankings and qualification for invitational events
- Securing medical treatment and physical rehabilitation facilities with lower risk of COVID-19 exposure

NBA Bubble Versus Non-Bubble Alternatives

There were no simple solutions for the many challenges facing sports organization managers aiming to restart operations. The idea of creating a protected environment in a biosecure bubble where athletes and staff were tested and quarantined to minimize risk of COVID-19 infections circulating in the bubble emerged as a potential solution. Many challenges remained including finding a suitable location and facilities that could be adapted for this specialized use, as well as changing the routines of athletes to fit the specialized facilities available. The NBA chose this approach to complete the 2019-20 season and maintain its broadcast and sponsorship agreements.

On June 4, 29 of the 30 teams in the NBA voted to proceed with a biosecure bubble plan. The ESPN Wide World of Sports complex at Disney World in Orlando, Florida and adjacent hotels were selected to host the games and broadcasts. To achieve the most secure possible implementation, the league crafted a 116-page rule book together with team doctors and medical experts to minimize infection risks for all those screened to enter the bubble. The rule book was not a set of guidelines; it was produced as a written agreement all participants were required to sign and included financial penalties and potential suspensions for non-compliance.

Rigorous testing to detect any COVID-19 infections among players and staff designated to work in the bubble setting before arrival at the Orlando facility was a cornerstone of the plan. This was followed by regular testing after entering the bubble and completing the mandatory quarantine there. Participants were encouraged to use sophisticated sensors to detect potential exposure to a COVID-19 infection. One was a wireless device that would send an alert if a close contact later tested positive for COVID-19. In addition, participants were offered a ring that would monitor temperature, heart rate, and other health metrics for changes that might be early warning signs of a COVID-19 infection. More rigorous medical checks by medical personnel were to be scheduled based on individual profiles.

The plan included detailed provisions for keeping the athletes rested and well fed. Each player had a private room at one of the Disney World hotels with many dining choices and access to the resort's golf courses, pools, and other recreation. During the playoffs, players were permitted to invite a guest who had agreed to the testing and quarantine requirements. Mask and safety practices based on CDC guidelines encouraged safe interactions between those present in the bubble.

The plan tried to rely on more extensive use of remote video support services, including telehealth consultations, to minimize the number of support staff on site. Each team was permitted 15 to 17 players, a public relations advisor, a digital content specialist, and up to 20 support staff. Teams arranged to share specialists such as therapists and nutritionists to get the best results. Broadcast professionals transmitted camera feeds to local broadcasters who aired games of teams from their area and arranged for remote commentary, reducing the need for personnel within the bubble.

Only 22 of the 30 teams in the NBA were asked to compete in games at the NBA bubble. Eight teams had not accumulated enough wins to potentially compete in the NBA playoffs. Excluding these eight teams made the details of accommodating and supervising the players more manageable and reduced the number of broadcast professionals needed in the bubble. Five players on teams invited to Orlando to complete the season opted out for personal reasons and took unpaid leaves. Avery Bradley of the Los Angeles Lakers did not want to take any chance that he might transmit a COVID-19 infection to his oldest child, who had previously been diagnosed with respiratory health problems. Two additional players tested positive for COVID-19 upon their arrival in Orlando before entering the bubble and were isolated before the infections could spread further.

Restarting the 2019-20 season in the Orlando bubble required a combination of flexibility and determination. Quarters were shortened from 12 minutes to 10 minutes in the exhibition games to support a transition back to the court for players who had not been training regularly together for four months. Each team played eight regular season games from the original 2019-20 season schedule to select the 16 teams to compete in the playoffs.

No spectators were allowed at games. The creative team introduced enhanced audio features to give the television audience at home a more stadium-like viewing experience. In addition, the NBA worked with the Microsoft Teams platform to show fans watching games and cheering their team on big screens.

The basketball competitions proceeded in line with expectations from earlier in the season. The Los Angeles Lakers won their 17th NBA Championship, defeating the Miami Heat on October 12. The revised playoff schedule made this the longest season in NBA history. In total, the NBA bubble operated for just over three months.

The NBA restart plan was complicated, but it worked well. The 2019-20 schedule was completed with modifications as necessary and, most importantly, there was not a single case of COVID-19 infection in the bubble during the entire period. The financial results were difficult but manageable; they kept key elements of NBA business operations intact so that the league could plan to continue in the future. The NBA reported that total expenditures for operating the bubble reached $190 million and enabled the league to take in $1.5 billion in broadcast and sponsorship revenues. The lack of ticketing revenues, typically 40 percent of total revenues for an NBA team, was reflected in an overall decline of 10 percent in revenues from the previous season.

The NBA bubble model was adopted by several other sports organizations as a manageable solution for continuing operations during a global health crisis. But implementation was not uniformly easy. Major League Soccer (MLS) established a bubble in the ESPN Wide World of Sports at Disney World in Orlando and was confronted with player COVID-19 infections that scrambled the schedule.

MLS organized its restart as a special event, branded as the "MLS Is Back Tournament." This gave the league's own management team more control over the details of implementation and scheduling. Unlike then NBA, where the number of COVID-19 infections detected before arrival at the Orlando bubble did not affect operations, the infection rates reported at two MLS tournament teams were so high that they could not compete as originally planned. FC Dallas had a total of ten players plus one coach test positive and the team was excluded from the tournament. Before arriving at the Orlando bubble, Nashville SC reported five players testing positive. Nashville was not immediately excluded from the tournament, but its first match was postponed indefinitely, with a ripple effect on the rest of the schedule. When no scheduling solution could match facility availability, Nashville had to withdraw from the tournament and the tournament schedule was reduced by three matches.

The "MLS Is Back Tournament" faced an additional hurdle arranging for Canadian teams from Toronto and Vancouver to compete. The USA – Canada border was closed to non-essential travel and Canadians have a 180-day-a-year residency requirement to retain their access to Canada's national health insurance system. For this challenge, a biosecure bubble with no player travel also emerged as the most workable option.

MLS was able to implement biosecure bubble guidelines comparable to the NBA and draw upon the experience the Disney staff had accumulated with NBA teams for accommodation and training to keep the players fit and healthy. The tournament concluded as planned with a final on August 11. The biosecure bubble had achieved the important objectives of keeping players active and competitive while providing quality live sports content for broadcast partners. The results were impressive enough that the tournament was distinguished with Sports Business Journal's "Sports Event of the Year" award. The momentum supported a restart of a shortened 2020 MLS season in home stadiums designed for a "made for television" format.

The financial pain of presenting matches without ticket and merchandising revenues combined with the additional expense of medical testing and operating a biosecure bubble was substantial. At the end of the 2020 season, MLS Commissioner Dan Garber reported that the combined revenues of MLS and its 26 active clubs were almost $1 billion less in 2020 than 2019. Players accepted a uniform 5% pay cut and 20% of support staff positions were cut. Garber admitted candidly that MLS could not absorb such large losses for two consecutive seasons.

Ultimately, the MLS restart strategy gave the organization enough leeway to maintain operations and build for the future. In April 2021, MLS announced a 5-year sponsorship arrangement with P&G. This focused on promoting both the P&G consumer product brands and the MLS brand. The financial package was estimated at $100 million, but this program offered the additional advantage of building interest in MLS with hundreds of millions of P&G customers.

The National Hockey League (NHL) also selected a biosecure bubble as a foundation of its restart strategy. The regular 2019-20 season had been suspended March 12 before the regional playoffs and Stanley Cup finals could take place. The NHL pursued a "zero COVID" strategy and it worked. Not a single player or support staff member experienced a positive COVID-19 test during the entire operation of the bubble from July 26 to September 28.

The NHL's selection of facilities was strongly influenced by community incidence of COVID-19 infections. Toronto and Edmonton in Canada won on that basis. Canada had closed its border with the US to non-essential travel and mandated a 14-day quarantine for international arrivals. Therefore, the "zero COVID" strategy was designed to be so rigorous that the local health authorities would grant a quarantine exemption.

The facilities selected supported a high degree of distancing from any outside infection risks. Both cities had ice sports arenas connected to hotels which served as accommodation and training facilities for all 26 teams.

The NHL restart strategy achieved key objectives of fulfilling multi-year broadcast contracts and keeping players conditioned for elite competition. But presenting a winter sport in summer competing for audience attention with MLB and NFL broadcasts was unprecedented and yielded disappointing results. The US television audience for the Stanley Cup finals declined by 61 percent compared to the 2019 series. The NHL earned positive reviews from broadcast professionals for its approach to empty spectator stands with sophisticated crowd sound effects and camera footage designed to replicate a spectator's experience.

"Zero-COVID" also resulted in zero income from on-site spectator revenues which had reached $20 million for the previous year's Stanley Cup final. Revenues from the regular season played before the pandemic buffered the financial difficulty for the NHL. Annual operating income declined by 68 percent but was still in the profitable zone at $250 million. However, the high-end estimate of future losses from an entire season played without spectators was $1 billion.

Testing Alternatives

Major League Baseball evaluated multiple alternatives for conducting the 2020 season as safely as possible in the midst of the COVID-19 Pandemic.

With a typical team roster of 40 players and 30 teams, plus an entire season to play, a biosecure bubble did not appear feasible. The alternatives left the professionals of the league vulnerable to COVID-19 infections from many directions, including travel, family interactions, team practices, and contacts with staff members. The result was very high infection rates that reverberated through frequent rescheduling challenges and large-scale quarantines.

A large part of the 2020 baseball season was simply cancelled. The College World Series planned for Omaha, the World Baseball Classic scheduled for a three nation tour, the MLB All-Star Game set for Dodger Stadium, and the entire Minor League Baseball schedule did not take place at all. Series scheduled to take place in front of fans in Mexico City and Puerto Rico were likewise cut from the 2020 schedule with no replacements. The MLB draft was postponed from June to July and downsized, including a provision that converted signing bonuses to deferred compensation.

MLB coordinated with team owners and players representatives to try to craft a schedule that would apply conventional practices in testing and contact tracing to isolate COVID-19 infections and permit healthy players and staff to stage baseball games in MLB team ballparks. The ideal outcome would be a win-win scenario with owners able to hold on to some broadcast and sponsorship revenues and players able to earn part of their salaries. The plan would enable most teams to maintain almost all skilled staff and avoid the additional challenge of recruiting and retraining staff. An additional position was added to all 30 MLB teams. That was the senior staff position of compliance officer for MLB's COVID-19 protocols.

Navigating the details of player compensation agreements faced hurdles from multiple directions. Some mass market services such the UPS and FedEx delivery services could – and did – implement contract changes based on "force majeure" circumstances beyond their control because of the COVID-19 Pandemic. But sports team owners recognized the importance of trusting relationships with players and the importance of player morale to winning games. Representatives of the players union were consulted regarding the practical details of implementing COVID-19 safety practices, as well as modifying benefits and compensation to accommodate a shorter season. The changes included provisions for pro-rating compensation and allowing players to opt out of playing the 2020 season. Several players and a dozen umpires ultimately chose to opt out of the 2020 season.

Medical privacy rules are different in different states, so the full extent of COVID-19 infections impacting the 2020 season is not certain. Several players voluntarily disclosed their COVID-19 infection experiences and sports journalists complied lists of players reported on injury lists for undisclosed reasons with no known physical injury. The latter were widely assumed to be COVID-19 infections. In just the first week of the shortened season that began on July 23, there were 34 of these players reported on injury lists for undisclosed reasons. In addition, 17 players from the Miami Marlins, 3 from the St. Louis Cardinals, and 5 from other MLB teams could not play because of positive COVID-19 test results. Effectively five percent of the player capacity in the league was incapacitated by COVID-19 infections in the first week of the season.

The rescheduling challenge increased. At the halfway point of the shortened 2020 season, a total of 43 games from the original schedule had already been postponed in accordance with MLB's testing and quarantine protocols. The efforts the league had made to compose a schedule that reduced travel between cities and effectively reduce the total number of contacts that individual players also resulted in a situation where 90 percent of the postponements involved doubleheaders or series of three or four games.

Perseverance became a key success factor in carrying on with the 2020 season and responding to extraordinary obstacles. While MLB management had indicated its readiness to suspend the 2020 season if the health risks worsened dramatically, the season was completed and capped by the traditional World Series. The Los Angeles Dodgers won the championship with a win over the Tampa Bay Rays on October 26.

There were no exceptional wins on the financial side of the MLB restart, where simply surviving had become an ambitious goal. According to Forbes' annual survey of MLB team financial results, all 30 MLB teams lost money in the 2020 season and total losses for all 30 teams combined reached $1 billion. Major loss drivers included:

- No spectator ticket revenues, except for a very few games where local health conditions permitted a limited number of spectators

- Additional costs of COVID-19 testing and health protocol compliance
- Broadcast fee shortfalls for games not played due to the shortened season
- Stadium maintenance and financing costs
- Stadium rental income losses due to nearly universal prohibitions of large gatherings

Despite these challenges, MLB television and streaming revenues increased modestly as audiences encouraged to stay at home tuned in. 2020 was a terrible year, but the MLB restart program preserved the foundations for MLB to return to profitability in the future.

The National Football League (NFL) faced many of the same challenges as MLB in ensuring player safety and modifying plans to accommodate the rigors of COVID-19 prevention. But it had the latitude of more time to develop and implement solutions for the 2020-21 season and fewer total games to play spread out over a longer period. The regular season schedule for NFL teams was 16 games in a 17-week time frame, while the shortened 2020 season for MLB teams required 60 games.

Testing, contact tracing, and quarantine became the fundamental approach to limiting COVID-19 infections among NFL players and staff. Players and the staff members they worked with in person were tested for COVID-19 infections every day. The additional costs of testing reached $100 million for the 32 teams together. Players who tested positive were isolated for a minimum of 10 days and put on a reserved injured list throughout their recovery. The NFL also offered players the choice of opting not to play the 2020 season and reactivating their contracts in the 2021 season. A total of 67 NFL players ultimately chose to opt out.

The NFL COVID-19 protocols were exceptional in the extent to which they demanded that players reduce the risk of contracting COVID-19 in their private lives. The focus was on avoiding indoor social settings where the risk of COVID-19 infection was judged to be higher by the NFL's medical experts.

While COVID-19 testing identified both individual infections and wider outbreaks at NFL teams, no games needed to be cancelled entirely from the schedule. But postponements demanded schedule changes, accommodated by a buffer week and weekday games. The Tennessee Titans experienced the first outbreak putting twelve players on the reserve list in early October. A game between the New England Patriots and Kansas City Chiefs was postponed from Sunday, October 4 to the evening of October 5 to enable comprehensive testing of all players after single cases of COVID-19 on the squads of each team.

Only 19 of the 32 teams in the NFL were able to accommodate any spectators at home games in the 2020 season. It became possible to work with local health agencies near some stadiums to enable limited attendance with social distancing in select regions where COVID-19 was not spreading so rapidly that the local health care system was at risk of exhausting capacity. Tampa Bay and Jacksonville were able to operate at close to one-quarter capacity while the Miami Dolphins accommodated 20 percent of the attendance of the 2019 season. Average spectator attendance at the 19 NFL team stadiums with limited seating was only 10 percent of the previous season. The league's total season attendance of 1.2 million was just 7.3 percent of the 2019 season.

The decline in the NFL's US television audience was also exceptional. Nielson estimated total television and live streaming viewing of the February 2021 Super Bowl at 96.4 million, down 20 million from the peak audience reached in 2015. Advertisers absorbed the loss entirely, since the Super Bowl does not guarantee a minimum viewing audience, unlike most other sports broadcasts.

The massive drop in ticket revenues put pressure on NFL team finances. This motivated the teams to modify agreements with players' representatives. Their goal was to survive 2020 to profit from better opportunities in the future. The estimated decline of ticket and concession revenues reached $2.8 billion so reducing player compensation could only cushion the financial impact. Each team was allowed to reduce total player compensation by up to $20 million and players agreed that they would not be paid if the pandemic forced the 2020 season to stop. That left team owners to reduce operating expenses, seek more sponsorship dollars or draw down on their financial reserves to make up revenue shortfalls. The total revenue decline reported by the NFL and its 32 teams for the 2020 season was $4 billion compared to the 2019 season, when total revenues reached $16 billion. Over $1 billion in losses resulted from loss of stadium rental income normally generated by other spectator events.

A Global Challenge

While the COVID-19 pandemic caused financial losses at leading sports organizations in the United States that were painful, leagues and teams in other markets faced tough challenges simply to survive. UEFA reported that the combined losses of professional football clubs in Europe reached 9 billion Euros for the 2020-21 season.

The estimated combined losses of the 20 teams in France's top tier Ligue 1 for the 2020-21 season were 1.3 billion Euros, over $1.5 billion. An international consortium that had committed to pay 780 million Euros for 80 percent of the games broadcast for four seasons through 2024 collapsed. The broadcast rights were then sold for only 35 million Euros for the pandemic challenged 2020-21 season. The financial pressure was set to continue for years since the alternative offers for broadcast rights came in at significantly lower figures.

Unlike the top tier of English football clubs and Germany's Bundesliga, France's professional football teams had totally cancelled the remaining games scheduled for the 2019-20 season. Ligue 1 used the results of average points scored per match to finalize the rankings for the season and Paris St. Germain was honored with the champion's title. The Belgian Pro League likewise cancelled the remainder of the 2019-20 season.

The English Premier League (EPL) determined to play the rest of the 2019-20 season after a 100-day suspension with COVID-19 precautions packaged as "Project Restart." No spectators were allowed and a maximum of 300 athletes, support staff, and broadcast professionals were permitted to access the playing areas. Matches took place in neutral stadiums selected to minimize the risk of exposure to COVID-19 further away from areas with high infection rates. The precautions worked and the infection rates reported were markedly lower than in the general population. In the first series of tests when training resumed in mid-May, just six players and staff of 748 tested positive for COVID-19. There were an additional eight positive results in 15,600 tests conducted during the restart season. No fatalities, hospitalizations, or secondary infections were reported.

Adapting to the pandemic required the Premier League clubs to redesign their strategy for broadcasting and streaming matches. The restart schedule was customized to reach the largest audiences possible.

Manchester City's match against Southampton on BBC Sport set a new audience record of 5.7 million. Amazon promoted four matches on its online gaming platform, Twitch. The matches were free to view but gave Amazon a valuable advertising and marketing asset and boosted the Premier League's visibility with the youthful demographic most active on Twitch. The initiative worked and enabled Twitch to expand its live streaming of sports in other markets. The Project Restart goal of expanding the audience for EPL achieved the longer- term benefit of keeping renewal rates for broadcast rights contracts high, despite the downward pressure on broadcast rights experienced by many other leagues.

Success in operations and marketing helped EPL limit financial losses as it completed the 2020 season, but these were still painful. The Sports Business Group at Deloitte Consulting reported that 75 percent of the EPL clubs lost money during the 2019-20 season and that the cumulative pre-tax loss reached almost one billion pounds, over $1.3 billion. As in other professional sports, loss of ticketing and concession revenues were worsened by the additional costs of implementing strict COVID-19 prevention measures.

The 42 teams in Spain's La Liga professional football organization also had to manage substantial revenue declines. Loss of ticketing revenue and game day merchandising pushed combined revenues down by 600 million Euros compared to the 2019-20 season. In the case of La Liga, a system of uniform spending cuts had already been agreed to by member clubs in 2013. FC Barcelona arranged a stopgap solution by persuading its top paid players to defer most of their normal salaries for the 2020-21 season for repayment in installments in future years. Only Gerard Pique, the owner of a League 3 team, agreed to an actual pay cut without reimbursement in the future. The player payment obligations pushed FC Barcelona's total debt close to one-half billion Euros, a sum that will constrain capacity to make new investments and recruit talent for years into the future. The other La Liga teams will be managing similar debt obligations and pressures to limit investments in future growth.

The 20 teams in Italy's Serie A football league also experienced financial setbacks that will extend for years in the future. Qatar based BeIN Sports did not renew its $85 million annual contract for Middle East regional broadcast rights and the price per game domestic broadcasters agreed to pay declined. Part of this reflected the long-term shift of advertising spending from broadcast television to social media sites, but the decline was exacerbated by the pandemic. This made maintaining fan interest a greater challenge. Like their counterparts in U.S. professional sports, these top tier international clubs also had increased spending for player testing and health care management, causing further losses.

The Formula 1 international auto racing circuit had the additional challenge of planning its restart across multiple countries where limitations caused by the COVID-19 Pandemic differed greatly and changed frequently. Formula 1 crafted a restart plan designed to support presentations for television audiences and limit contacts that could risk exposure to COVID-19. The summer 2020 restart was based on eight races in Europe, close to Formula 1's London headquarters and the operational bases of the teams.

A key element of Formula 1's plan for COVID-19 prevention was reducing the scale of staffing at events, but the numbers found to be essential to stage and broadcast a race remained exceptionally high compared to other sports. Formula 1 management limited each team to 80 support staff, 50 less than in the previous year. On-site broadcast teams were reduced to 60 from 250 in the previous year. Altogether, the number of individuals working on-site in each race reached 2,000. That figure was more than six times the upper limit established by the Premier League for its matches and was ultimately too large for traditional trace and isolate practices to prevent outbreaks.

Formula 1 implemented other measures to reduce the risk of COVID-19 transmission. All participants were tested before departure and frequently once they were on site. Formula 1 organized "sealed travel" with charter transport to limit contacts with the traveling public. Teams were requested to keep their contacts within each team and not interact with each other. Policies were carefully coordinated with local health authorities and designed to be modified if local outbreaks occurred.

Formula 1's return to the sports broadcast calendar was a success, but its COVID-19 containment strategy was not. One-third of the circuit's drivers tested positive for COVID-19 and had to self-isolate during the first six months of the season: Sergio Perez, Lance Stroll, Lewis Hamilton, Lando Norris, Charles Leclerc and Pierre Gasly. Three teams – McLaren,

Mercedes, and Williams – reported significant outbreaks affecting multiple staff members. These outbreaks required others who had been in close contact to self-isolate and managers to scramble to find qualified replacements.

The International Swimming League (ISL) designed its restart around a biosecure bubble concept and showed that it was possible to present international sports competitions safely during the COVID-19 pandemic, even if it was difficult. At the end of its six-week season in 2020, ISL reported that not a single swimmer competing had tested positive for COVID-19.

The ISL bubble provided a practical model for medium-sized sports organizations that do not have access to the multi-billion dollar budgets of top sports leagues. The biosecure facility was located on an island in the Danube River, close to the Budapest International Airport. COVID-19 testing before departure and after arrival made reasonably sure that no COVID-19 infections ever entered the bubble and testing continued daily throughout the six weeks of trials and competitions. All athletes, support staff, and broadcast crews were accommodated in single rooms at two hotels on the island. All swimmers had access to training and conditioning facilities and swim practice carefully scheduled to permit social distancing. There were some recreational options similar to athlete's villages at other sports events and the athletes found that there were training advantages to staying in one facility for an extended period and avoiding long trips to international meets. The televised competitions took place without spectators in the nearby Duna Arena.

ISL's restart strategy demonstrated strengths. The six weeks of competition achieved nine new world records. Caeleb Dressel set individual world records in the 50 meter Freestyle, 100 meter Butterfly, and 100 meter Individual Medley, Adam Peaty set two successive records in the 100 meter Breaststroke, Kliment Kolesnikov the 100 meter Backstroke and Kira Touissant in the 50 meter Backstroke. The Cali Condors women's team set a new record in the 400 meter medley relay.

ISL's management highlighted a key business objective of their restart plan that influenced al of the sports organizations which considered choices for resuming competitions rather than cancelling them outright. That objective was momentum. The investment in time and money to recruit staff and athletes, engage fans on social media and other channels, develop broadcast plans with broadcast partners and simply get access to broadcast channels in key markets is substantial. Walking away from these competitive advantages and trying to rebuild them years later involves risks that talent and business partnerships of similar caliber will not be readily available.

ISL's restart plan maintained the essential strengths to continue the competitions in a third season. The series took place in Naples, Italy in August 2021 and was broadcast by networks in 140 countries.

The Indian Premier League's (IPL) professional cricket restart strategy attracted international attention that matched its status as the professional sports league paying the highest compensation per game to players. It was a distinctively different approach, but not one that would not be easy to replicate. The original schedule for games to be played in front of spectators in India in spring 2020 had to be cancelled in line with an extended nationwide lockdown designed to prevent the spread of COVID-19. The lockdown impacted all sports competitions in India and the positive example of a league that could manage to restart would boost the image of all sports and provide the television audience with live sports once again.

IPL management decided to move the rescheduled 2020 season to the United Arab Emirates which had reopened to international arrivals on July 7 and had both cricket grounds and hotels available for a sports event on this scale. An unusual circumstance made this possible. Dubai had been scheduled to host the 2020 World Expo, which had been postponed by one year following the start of the Pandemic and entire facilities which had been booked for Expo staff and visitors were now available. This supported a limited biosecure bubble plan. Players screened for COVID-19 trained and competed at isolated facilities and traveled between cricket grounds in charter transport. The IPL restart program averted financial disaster and kept long-term broadcast and sponsorship agreements intact.

The Great Outdoors

Outdoor sports faced fewer obstacles to restarting during the COVID-19 Pandemic because of findings that transmission of infections outdoors was measurably lower – or even marginal – compared to indoor sports settings. Studies by the Technical University of Berlin showed substantial dilution of contagious viruses in outdoor settings and determined the risk of infection in outdoor sports was very low. That left multiple challenges in accommodating athletes, managing training facilities, and organizing support services like broadcast centers and food services, but most organizers found workable solutions that allowed 2020 competitions to be rescheduled and not cancelled. For most outdoor sports, this produced the additional advantages of growing both audiences and amateur participation in their sport.

While the COVID-19 pandemic wreaked havoc on the operations and finances of sports played in stadiums and arenas, many outdoor sports were able to adjust their practices to limit the risk of COVID-19 outbreaks and continue with planned competitions. The standout was the ninth Vendee Globe, a sailing race around the world by individual competitors with no crew which takes place every four years. Traditional festivities at the start and finish of the event could not take place because large gatherings were prohibited in France, but the competition itself took place with no major changes.

Vendee Globe's distinction as a live sports event during a year when many planned sports events were cancelled or postponed supported substantial audience growth and rewarded its sponsors with greater visibility. The volume of videos viewed on YouTube was almost seven times the figure from the previous edition in 2016 and digital media viewership increased even further with an entirely new Instagram channel achieving 2.5 million views. Combined social media following grew 135 percent. Dedicated television programming reported 54 percent growth over 2016.

The largest and most prestigious international sailing competition, the America's Cup, had the additional advantage that the host country, New Zealand, had effectively closed its borders early enough to remain almost free of COVID-19 infections. Local health authorities managed an alert system that imposed temporary restrictions in areas where small outbreaks occurred. International spectators could not travel to the America's Cup and international crews had to complete rigorous testing and quarantine requirements, but most training and competition proceeded as planned through the season, with races from December 2020 to

March 2021. No COVID-19 infections were reported among competitors, staff, or spectators.

International audiences appreciated the opportunity to watch a world class sporting event with a traditional celebratory atmosphere. The 36th America's Cup won the "Most Successful Sports Event Broadcast" award at Sports Business Awards 2021. Audience growth was spectacular and provided sponsors with exceptional value. The combined television and streaming audience reached 941 million, 82 percent greater than the 2018 FIFA Men's World Cup final and over six times larger than the February 2021 NFL Super Bowl. The audience in the core group of dedicated viewers who watched ten or more races reached 68.2 million. Audience gains also brought increases in social media following with 715 million posts viewed during the four months of races. The live audience was effectively limited to New Zealand residents and was reported at 280,000.

The more favorable environment for sailing helped the newly launched SailGP global yacht race series avoid cancellation of its second season, but postponement was unavoidable. Unlike Vendee Globe and the America's Cup, which use onshore operations in a single country, the SailGP concept was designed to have eight separate competitions in different international locations. The frequency and uncertainty of international travel restrictions and widespread use of quarantines for arriving international visitors made the original plan for the second season in 2020 unfeasible. But the organizers were ultimately able to craft a schedule that accommodated a world learning to live with COVID-19. They restarted the series in Bermuda in April 2021.

Professional golf managers benefitted from measurably lower COVID-19 infection risks in socially distanced outdoor sports, but still had challenges reorganizing support and accommodation services. Golf earned the distinction of being the first sport to organize an event in the US broadcast live on television since sports seasons were suspended in March 2020. The event "Taylor Made Driving Relief" was a doubles match between the team of Dustin Johnson and Rory McIlroy and the team of Rickie Fowler and Matthew Wolff. The broadcast was seen by 47.2 million viewers on NBC and the NBC Golf Channel in the US and Eurosport in Europe.

The Professional Golfers Association (PGA) developed a restart plan that relied on a combination of health monitoring and COVID-19 testing to find and isolate any COVID-19 infections so that an outbreak could be avoided. It published a series of guidelines that mirrored public health department recommendations for social distancing and hygiene. The PGA also organized travel facilities that gave players more choices to avoid contact with risk of COVID-19 infections.

Following the PGA's guidelines was mandatory on the golf course but voluntary off the golf course and had mixed results from a health management perspective. A summary of COVID-19 case reports by USAToday Golfweek showed that two dozen players or PGA Tour caddies tested positive for COVID-19 during the first eight months of the restarted season. All were unable to compete until they had recovered. The test results showed that about 5 percent of the players and caddies in the group tested positive, an infection rate about half of the general US population during this period. No fatalities were reported. The test and isolate strategy managed to avoid any contagious spread within the PGA community.

The professional golf restart plan involved ongoing adaptation to the global health crisis and difficult postponement decisions. The Ryder Cup between teams of golfers from the US and Europe, originally scheduled for September 2020, was postponed for one year. The traditional Master's tournament, originally scheduled for April was postponed to mid-November. Eight other tournaments on the 2020 schedule were postponed and ten were cancelled. This included six contests scheduled for courses in Canada, where 14-day quarantine requirements for international arrivals made it impossible to maintain the season schedule.

The LPGA series for top ranked female golfers made a major adjustment to its operations and held most of the remaining 2020 tournaments in the US after the season restarted on July 31. The notable exception was two tournaments held as originally scheduled in Scotland in August, when the area briefly reopened most activities in between lockdowns prompted by the first and second waves of COVID-19. The LPGA added two tournaments to the U.S. schedule to replace some of the opportunities lost by cancellation of planned events in Asia in autumn 2020.

The French Open of Golf, traditionally held in the spring, postponed the original 2020 schedule during France's first lockdown and was forced to announce another postponement in 2021, when France implemented another lockdown in May 2021. Organizers revamped the entire schedule, announcing that the next tournament would take place in September 2022 and the event would continue to take place in the autumn.

Professional cycling had two advantages to support a quick return to the international sports calendar. Non-track events were outdoors with lower infection risks and the financial model depended very little on revenues generated by spectators. Event organizers still faced major challenges moving cyclists and staff across borders to dozens of races in different countries and fine-tuning schedule changes to minimize conflicts on the sports broadcast calendar.

The complications of frequently changing international travel restrictions and quarantine requirements gave the cycling sports federation UCI almost no choice but to focus on races planned for continental Europe's Schengen Zone. These 26 countries normally permit travel across borders without border controls, although provisions for exceptions in emergencies resulted in temporary exceptions throughout the COVID-19 pandemic. Two races scheduled in Canada and one each in the United States, England, and China were removed from the calendar. Two of the most prestigious races, the Giro de Italia and Tour de France, took place on the originally planned courses and the likewise prestigious Vuelta de Espana took place on a shortened course. Daily testing and isolation protocols kept COVID-19 outbreaks from occurring.

UCI's recommendations for outdoor events encouraged emulating the lower risk environment of a bubble without the extraordinary restrictions of a bubble. The policies mandated social distancing and prohibited communal dining and changing facilities and arranged for separate access by different groups. The appointment of a race doctor, already a standard practice before the pandemic, became mandatory. The race doctor became responsible for reporting COVID-19 infections and transferring the patient to the nearest qualified treatment facility. This approach worked well enough so that there were no outbreaks requiring quarantines of groups or teams and the results of competition were not impacted by the pandemic, although isolated individual positive results required several cyclists to withdraw from competition.

By the end of the shortened season, community infection rates had risen in the second wave of infections to impact continental Europe, and the Amstel Gold Race in the Netherlands and Paris-Roubaix in France were cancelled on short notice.

While UCI was able to maintain the foundations of its elite racing program, give sponsors global visibility and provide broadcast partners with quality content, the financial pressure of cancelling so many events in one season pushed the organization below its operating breakeven point. But conservative cost control measures kept the damage to a minimum compared to the large losses reported by professional leagues in spectator sports. UCI's annual report for 2020 reported an operating loss of just under $2 million and reserves for future operations of $50 million. Losses were kept low by reducing the pay of senior executives and by implementing rolling furloughs of other staff which reduced expenses in proportion to the downsizing of the 2020 season. UCI established a task force to help teams competing on the World Tour survive financially and all made it through the season.

UCI's successful financial management enabled it to continue business development programs for future expansion. The launch of the UCI Pro Series for 2020 went ahead with additional COVID-19 safety precautions and modification of the original schedule, maintaining momentum for an ambitious 2021 season. UCI also stayed on schedule for the November 2021 launch of the UCI Track Cycling Series.

UCI's mass participation competition series, the Gran Fondo World Tour, was suspended following the annual Bathurst Cycling Classic March 15. The series restarted with an alternative that showed how enthusiasm and creativity can help in a crisis. The annual Franjo BTC City Marathon in Slovenia, originally scheduled for June 12 to 14 was postponed to 2021 to accommodate border closures and Slovenia's extended prohibition of mass gatherings. The local organizing committee put the course reservation for June 2020 to good work in a cleanup campaign, recruiting 200 supporters to cover the course with healthy social distancing and do their best to make the route safe and sanitary. COVID-19 infections were avoided, and the local organizing committee maintained the esprit de corps of the local supporters who make the event possible.

Business As Usual

While all sports event organizers had to make significant adjustments to present live sports and produce broadcasts, and most sports seasons were shortened in 2020, the global community of sports administration transformed itself online with minimal disruption and absolutely no COVID-19 outbreaks.

The MIT-Sloan Sports Analytics Conference in Boston on March 6 and 7 was the last sports business conference to take place in the U.S. before large gatherings were prohibited. SportCity took place in Lausanne the following week with strict attendance limits. Several events on the sports business calendar scheduled later in March had to be cancelled on short notice: the IHRSA Fitness Equipment Expo in San Diego, SXSW Sports in Austin, IEG World in Chicago, and the Sports Innovation 2020 Congress in Dusseldorf.

On March 25, the CAA World Congress of Sports presented its originally planned schedule of talks and workshops online following the original schedule, reaching its target audience of sports industry senior executives and financial institutions. This success validated the effectiveness of the switch online and the context of lockdowns in most countries made it a good alternative to postponements. Most other major sports business events followed the example:

- The SportTechie State of the Industry Conference
- Leaders Week New York 2020
- 2020 Sports Business Awards
- 2020 Intersport Brand Innovation Summit
- International Sports Convention 2020 London
- Europe Sports Tech Conference
- Coliseum Sports Venue Alliance Summits
- ISPO Munich, the world's largest trade fair for sports business

A few major sports business events took place in person with capped attendance and social distancing, including SoccerEx Europe 2020 in Portugal and SportBiz Europe in Spain. Global Sports Week adopted a hybrid format, setting up a socially distanced forum and broadcast center at the Eiffel Tower in Paris and letting viewers and some speakers connect to the platform over the Internet.

The quick transition to online presentation of sports business conferences had the additional advantage of providing the most current know-how on ways to continue operating sports events in the exceptional environment of travel restrictions and limits on holding events in person. This helped to keep valuable sports sponsorship arrangements in place as sports managers learned how to adapt their visibility and VIP introduction programs to digital media.

Sports leagues and federations also found workable solutions to move board meetings, press conferences, technical committee meetings and training programs online. The Global Association of International Sport Federations moved its annual meeting of sports federation executives online in November 2020 and retained the format for 2021. One federation, IBSF Bobsled, reported that changing international meetings to online conferences had reduced meeting expenses by 75 percent.

Maintaining valuable sports industry contacts online preserved the foundation for a return to in person meetings in 2021. The Gold's Gym Convention in Las Vegas in January started the trend and the Coliseum Sports Venue Alliance returned to its traditional location at Ascot in England in September.

A Case in Point: The London Marathon

Professional sports found solutions to restart their operations with made for television events that limited COVID-19 infection risks. Mass participation events like marathons with tens of thousands of competitors and hundreds of thousands of spectators could not simply copy these models. The London Marathon determined to find a solution and managed to become the first international marathon to restart after pandemic restrictions paused professional sports in March 2020.

London Marathon Events had originally scheduled the 2020 London Marathon for April 26 and announced on March 13 that the 2020 edition would be postponed to October 4 to accommodate public health safety measures. After different alternatives for holding the postponed event were evaluated, management chose a hybrid model using a closed course for elite runners and a virtual marathon for amateur and aspiring professional runners. This approach enabled it to fulfill key commitments to sponsors and broadcast partners, as well as keep valuable contacts with tens of thousands of runners who raise money for charities while they run. In addition to the 45,000 runners who had qualified and registered, 457,000 applied to compete in 2020. There is no application fee, but registration fees of UKL 49 for UK residents and UKL 99 for international runners provide a key source of financing for the event's operations.

London Marathon Events operates several different mass participation events as lead organizer, and it also supports other competitions outside its area as a technical consultant. It was able to draw on its experience advising a closed course marathon in Vienna in 2019 and had expertise to create a similar course for elite runners in St. James Park, with the iconic backdrop of Buckingham Palace. Simple temporary construction secured the area from spectators, who were encouraged to watch the event safely at home on television.

The organizers recruited 100 top ranked competitors in four categories – men's marathon, women's marathon, men's wheelchair, and women's wheelchair. The UK entrants could qualify for the rescheduled Tokyo 2020 Olympics marathon with superior results. Most of the elite competitors had to travel from international locations and organizers developed a plan to minimize risk of COVID-19 infection en route. All runners and their essential support staff were tested for COVID-19 before departure and on arrival. One runner and one coach were not able to participate after receiving positive test results.

The elite runners, support staff, broadcast crews, and venue management team had to stay 10 days in a biosecure bubble established for the event at a spacious hotel complex in suburban London. The self-contained facility had exercise and training areas on-site and provided all meals and accommodation. Testing under the supervision of event sponsor Abbot Laboratories continued and confirmed that there were zero COVID-19 infections in the bubble throughout the period.

The broadcast team found several techniques to make the novel format more engaging for television audiences. Two stationary rail cameras and four mobile motorbike mounted cameras allowed television viewers to see the runners as if they were next to the course. Traditional aerial coverage from helicopters showed the runners against the backdrop of iconic central London landmarks. Clips of virtual marathon runners broadened the appeal of the broadcast with a kaleidoscope of images from homes and parks where the individual runners competed for their own personal bests. The broadcast team provided camera feeds to international broadcast partners who integrated commentary in local languages in their home studios. A mobile phone app developed by sponsor TCS expanded the audience reach.

While the elite runners did not achieve any new world records, the virtual runners did. *The Guinness Book of World Records* distinguished the 2020 London Marathon as the largest virtual mass participation sports event in world history. Over 36,000 virtual runners completed 26 miles on the Marathon Day to qualify as finishers.

Following the strict "stay-at-home" lockdowns which occurred in the Spring of 2020, international sports federations and elite athlete training facilities developed sophisticated health protocols. They also adapted training programs to minimize the risk of COVID-19 outbreaks and resume rigorous athletic training.

Photo by Max Donner at the Swiss Cycling National Stadium, Grenchen, Switzerland, April 5, 2021.

Key Sources and References

Associated Press. January 31, 2021. "Tennis Tour Hardship Looms Beyond Australian Open, Says Lleyton Hewitt."

Associated Press. April 21, 2020. "Baseball Quietly Returns to South Korea as Games Begin Without Fans." *ESPN.com*. www.espn.com/mlb/story/_/id/29074958/baseball-quietly-returns-south-korea-games-begin-fans.

Bataglio, S. February 9, 2021. "21 Super Bowl Draws 96.4 Million TV and Streaming Viewers, Lowest Since 2007." *Los Angeles Times*.

Chakrabarty, S. July 29, 2020. "IPL 2020: How the UAE Will Save BCCI Millions of Dollars." *Indianexpress.com*.

Cyclingnews staff. January 29, 2021. "2021 Road Calendar COVID-19 Cancellations." *Cyclingnews.com*.

France 24 News Desk. February 2, 2021. "Bleeding Cash, Top French Football League Signs Stopgap TV Deal With Canal+."

Houston, M. January 27, 2021. "Volleyball Nations League to Be Held in a Bubble in 2021." *Insidethegames.biz*.

ISL News. November 20, 2020. "The Show Must Go On. Safely."

Jurejko, J. February 8, 2021. "Australian Open: Fans Back as Grand Slam Gets Under Way in Melbourne." *BBC Sport*.

Maine, D. January 25, 2021. "Australian Open 2021—How Players Are Adapting to Training in Quarantine." *ESPN.com*.

MLSsoccer staff. Thursday, June 24, 2021. "MLS Is Back Tournament Wins SBJ's Sports Event of the Year." *MLSsoccer.com*.

Murad, A. October 27, 2021. "Foreigners Rush to Buy Italian Football Clubs." *Financial Times*.

NFL.com staff, September 8, 2020. "A Comprehensive Approach to Safety During COVID-19." www.nfl.com/playerhealthandsafety/health-and-wellness/covid-19/a-comprehensive-approach-to-safety-during-covid-19?campaign=sp-pg-lp-ps-li-12013729.

Pennington, W. May 13, 2020. "PGA Tour Lays Out Plan to Restart." *New York Times*.

Raimondi, M. July 6, 2020. "UFC Fight Island to Feature Safe Zone, Increased Testing." *ESPN.com*. www.espn.com/mma/story/_/id/29420449/ufc-fight-island-feature-safe-zone-increased-testing.

Savary, D. February 1, 2021. "Face au Covid, le Tour de France s'est réinventé." *Sport + Tourisme*.

Stachura, M. April 7, 2021. "The Numbers Are Official: Golf's Surge in Popularity in 2020 Was Even Better Than Predicted. *GolfNews*.

Young. J. April 13, 2021. "Major League Soccer Lands a Top Corporate Sponsorship." *CNBC*. www.cnbc.com/2021/04/13/major-league-soccer-lands-top-corporate-sponsorship-procter-gamble.html.

CHAPTER 3

Marathon Race

Staying in the Game—At a High Cost

In the autumn of 2020, second waves of COVID-19 outbreaks swept the globe and prompted frequent restrictions on meetings, travel, and facilities. Sports leaders were compelled to pace themselves for a long distance run to be able to resume full operations with full spectator stands and a return to profitability in the future. In most cases, the most ambitious goal they could envision was to maintain a foundation of broadcast partners, fan supporter groups, and dedicated staff to be able to keep athletes competitive and rebuild when opportunities emerged in the future. The year ahead began to look like a marathon race where simply crossing the finish line would be celebrated as a success. Not all made it across the finish line. Many event series were entirely eliminated, and many smaller teams discontinued operations.

Australia's exceptional ability to keep most domestic activities open during the COVID-19 pandemic supported optimism that the annual Australian Open Grand Slam tennis tournament would take place again in the winter of 2021. Finding solutions and carrying out the plan was nonetheless complicated and controversial. The effort was rewarded with two weeks of events that completely contained all infections found among international arrivals and zero community transmission.

Australia's "zero-COVID" policy used stringent border controls, quarantines for international arrivals, and targeted lockdowns to keep COVID-19 from spreading in 2020 and 2021. All international arrivals were required to quarantine for 14 days in a government supervised facility and continue to test negative. Occasional cases entered the community, often linked to the transport of international arrivals. However, the subsequent strict lockdowns kept total reported cases to around 28,500 and fatalities under 1,000 in 2020.

Limits on international arrivals were so strict that many Australian citizens had lengthy waits for opportunities to return. Making additional capacity available for international tennis players, family members, and staff would take even more resources. The leaders of Victoria state, where the Melbourne tournament was scheduled, were determined to move forward. The featured goal was to demonstrate how it could be possible to safely produce a major international sports event during a global pandemic. Organizers also recognized that cancelling the event could result in the prestigious Grand Slam tournament moving to another host country for the January–February period.

Organizers chose two major changes to implement a COVID-19 prevention strategy. First, the qualifying tournaments for international players were held in Qatar, which reduced the number of places needed in Australian quarantine. Second, the start of the tournament was moved three weeks from its original date in mid-January to enable a 14-day quarantine for all international players.

The quarantine restrictions for the international players who tested negative for COVID-19 were tough, and they were even tougher for the two who tested positive for COVID-19 on arrival or were classified as close contacts. All players and an accompanying guest were limited to their hotel rooms, with five hours of practice at supervised facilities separated from the rest of Melbourne. But 72 players arrived on one of three flights where another passenger not participating in the tournament had tested positive for COVID-19 on arrival. These 72 players were completely confined to their hotel rooms with no outside practice for 14 days. The exceptional challenge created a social media phenomenon. Fans could see their favorite players improvising training regimens to practice serves and volleys inside a hotel room smaller than a viewer's apartment.

The rigorous quarantine requirements for tennis players were the same as for rugby players traveling from outside Australia for the Ron Massey Cup, cricket players for the Ashes Tournament, and surfers for the Rip Curl Newcastle Cup.

The COVID-19 control program in the Melbourne Park spectator area tried to make social distancing comfortable. Maximum attendance was limited to under 50 percent of total seating, with a cap of 30,000 spectators a day. Spectators were admitted to one of three separate zones to facilitate contact tracing if a spectator tested positive for COVID-19 afterward. That possibility also made prospective attendees think twice about attending in person and taking a chance that they would have to isolate for 14 days if another attendee in the zone tested positive.

On the fifth day of the 2021 Australian Open, a single case of COVID-19 traced to a worker in a quarantine hotel prompted an immediate five-day lockdown of the entire state of Victoria. The tournament had to switch to "Plan B"—a biosecure bubble for the athletes shuttled between stadiums, training areas, and hotels with no outside contacts. The matches took place as scheduled in a "made-for-television" format.

The Australian Open kept its status as one of four prestigious "Grand Slam" tournaments but still had significant declines in television viewing audiences to contend with. The U.S. broadcaster ESPN reported that viewership declined 27 percent from 2020. This was not as severe as the 40 percent decline in the television audience for the U.S. Open in September 2020, but it was beyond the threshold for automatic advertiser refunds. The local television audience in Australia declined by 30 percent, and local broadcaster Channel Nine negotiated a 10 percent reduction in its broadcast rights fee.

Digital media made up some of the viewer losses impacting the television audience but not the financial losses. Australian Open content was viewed 150 million times on Twitter, 88.8 million times on Instagram, and 65.9 million times on Facebook. However, the advertising revenue generated went to the social media giants and not to the event's organizer, Tennis Australia.

Revenue losses from spectator capacity limits were compounded by refunds for tickets during the five-day lockdown and reductions in the fees charged to broadcasters. When the final accounting for the two-week event, including additional quarantine and safety costs, was completed, the financial loss reached US$70 million. The losses from the 2021 tournament exhausted Tennis Australia's reserves of approximately $55 million and forced the host organization to draw on a line of credit to continue operations in 2022.

The International Ice Hockey Federation (IIHF) overcame many challenges to be able to organize a few selected international competitions so that it could remain viable in the future. The series of lockdowns and travel bans that started in the winter of 2020 conflicted with the original schedule for the flagship World Championships of the 2020 season. First, the Halifax Women's World Championship was cancelled, and then the Men's World Championship planned for Zurich, Switzerland, was also cancelled. Ultimately, all eight of the championship series in four men's divisions were cancelled, not postponed, and a total of 19 events were cancelled.

The IIHF was able to use event cancellation insurance and some cost control measures to maintain its most essential operations, keep its expert staff on its payroll, and provide some funding to national federations to help them stay viable during this difficult period. Nonetheless, the operating loss for the season was just over CHF 4 million, about $4.25 million. That left IIHF with over $35 million in reserves at the end of the season, a key resource for somehow managing to get through the difficult year that followed.

The IIHF established an expert group to develop a workable solution for the 2020–2021 season. The group's assignment was to evaluate the feasibility of each event from financial, medical, marketing, player development, legal, event operations, and local community relations perspectives.

The IIHF World Championships were also designated Olympic-qualifying events for the 2022 Winter Olympics. Fulfilling this role required streamlining the 2020–2021 event calendar. At the same time, accommodating travel restrictions and a series of NHL postponements that extended the season to May 11 narrowed the choices available. The final result was extreme—28 of the 32 events planned for the season were cancelled. That also meant sacrificing the efforts of 28 host community organizations and many opportunities for players and coaches to accumulate relevant experience. It also meant disappointing fans and refunding their ticket purchases.

The IIHF selected four series to help maintain relations with its fan base, sponsors, and business partners and provide at least some professional opportunities for key support staff whose expertise would be essential for a full-scale restart in the future. These were the Ice Hockey Men's World Championship, the Men's World Junior Championship, the Ice Hockey Women's World Championship, and the Ice Hockey Men's Under-18 World Championship.

The IIHF Men's World Junior Championship tested the limits of what was possible for international sports during the peak of a global pandemic. Edmonton had already been selected to co-host the tournament with another Canadian city, Red Deer. The relative success of the NHL bubble in Edmonton built confidence that this approach would also work for a smaller IIHF tournament. The facility of Rogers Place and the connected hotel needed only minor modifications, and the local host committee agreed to assume responsibility for COVID-19 testing and prevention.

While the biosecure bubble successfully prevented any new COVID-19 infections from starting inside the bubble, the incidence of COVID-19 infections detected in pretravel and pretournament screenings was very high. Two positive COVID-19 tests among Canadian players caused the entire team to be quarantined for 14 days. Nine players from the German team tested positive for COVID-19 after their arrival in Edmonton and were quarantined before being permitted to enter the biosecure bubble. Four players of the Swedish team, along with the head coach, remained in Sweden after testing positive for COVID-19 prior to departure for Canada. In addition, two weeks before the start of the tournament, IIHF President Rene Fasel and IIHF General Secretary Horst Lichtner tested positive for COVID-19 and had to isolate for two weeks in Switzerland.

The IIHF Men's World Junior Championship management overcame the revenue loss from zero spectators by raising funds directly from the large television audience (confined in their homes over the Christmas—New Year's Holiday). An online lottery for Canadian television viewers netted US$15 million and largely covered the costs of hosting the tournament. The domestic Canadian audience reached 13.5 million, or 36 percent of Canada's total population, making the tournament the top-ranked broadcast during the period. The international television audience topped 100 million.

Five months later, the IIHF continued to rely on a biosecure bubble approach for the IIHF Men's World Championship and Olympic Qualifier in Riga, Latvia. Athletes were confined to hotels with no visitors permitted, the two ice arenas hosting training and competition, and exclusive shuttles from six days before the start of the tournament until departure. The Italian team experienced a major COVID-19 outbreak before their scheduled arrival at the bubble, with a total of 15 cases, including head coach Greg Ireland and other staff. Young players from the development team were substituted, but Italy finished the tournament in last place.

The International Skating Union (ISU) also employed a biosecure bubble approach for its 2021 World Championship and Olympic Qualifier. The stakes were very high. The 2020 World Championship had to be cancelled because of COVID-19 lockdowns and travel bans, and the international competitions originally scheduled for the 2020–2021 season were also cancelled as the second wave of COVID-19 closed borders. The European Championships scheduled for Zagreb in January were cancelled after the arena was quickly converted into a temporary emergency hospital for COVID-19 patients.

The ISU had the distinction of being the most financially secure international sports federation, with reserves of over $300 million; if it could not find a way to deliver its 2021 World Championship, it would have undermined confidence that financially weaker sports organizations could overcome COVID-19 pandemic challenges. Event cancellation insurance helped and provided $2.1 million for cancellations in the 2019–2020 season. ISU's directors established a $5.2 million special crisis reserve to handle anticipated extraordinary expenses during the pandemic.

The ISU 2021 World Championships took place on the dates and at the location originally planned since the selection of Stockholm as the host city in 2018. Athletes and international officials were tested for COVID-19 upon arrival and confined to quarantine hotel facilities until a subsequent negative test result. Two skaters returned positive results and were quarantined outside the bubble. No spectators were allowed, so the event was produced in a broadcast format. This preserved ISU's broadcast rights income and held on to its loyal international television audience.

The International Skiing Federation (FIS) was able to proceed with most plans for the 2020–2021 winter season since all the sports competitions took place outdoors and venues had ample space for social distancing. This still required substantial modifications and partial downsizing. Almost all events took place within the 26-country "Schengen Zone" in Europe to reduce quarantine requirements for participants. In normal times, all athletes and staff could move across the borders of the 26 countries whenever they needed to; during the second wave of the COVID-19 pandemic, ad hoc quarantine requirements based on local health conditions meant some areas could not host events as planned. A dozen competitions were relocated, and eight other FIS events were eliminated:

- Zao, Japan Women's Ski Jumping World Cup, November 2020
- Lillehammer, Norway Cross Country World Cup, December 2020
- San Candido, Italy FIS Ski Cross World Cup, December 2020
- Copper Mountain, Colorado FIS Freeski, and Snowboard World Cup, December 2020
- Otepää, Estonia Nordic combined, January 2021
- Nove Mesto, Czechia Cross Country World Cup February 2021
- Lillehammer, Norway Raw Air Ski Jumping Tournament, March 2021
- Kvitfjell, Norway Alpine Men's World Cup, March 2021

Due to schedule changes, most competitions originally planned for the United States and Canada were relocated to continental European ski areas. Cortina, Italy, which had planned to host the March 2021 Alpine World Cup championships, arranged a postponement to March 2022. In addition, the Ski World Cup finals planned as a 2022 Winter Olympics test event in China were also cancelled. The financial burdens accumulated. Fewer events resulted in fewer event broadcast contracts. Regional restrictions on spectators at sports events cut this source of revenue.

Expenses remained close to prepandemic levels. Average prize money winnings for the Top 20 of the 2020–2021 season increased modestly from the prepandemic 2018–2019 season. In the FIS Ski World Cup, that amounted to an average of $180,000 for men and $190,000 for women.

Despite many challenges, the ski industry was also able to move forward with modest global expansion. A new world class ski resort opened in the small country of Andorra. And Shanghai, China, presented its first ever cross-country skiing competition.

The International Handball Federation held its January 2021 World Championships and Olympic Qualifier in Egypt as planned and as originally scheduled. The organizing committee decided to use a modified bubble approach at three separate campuses for broadcast audiences and use testing to limit the spread of COVID. The approach avoided an outbreak of COVID in the general population, but the competition schedule was disrupted. Many athletes found the plan difficult to adapt to their training and team regimens.

Solutions found by some sports organizations to somehow move forward with select events despite the burdens posed by the pandemic encouraged others to try out strategies that had worked. Equestrian enthusiasts adapted the fundraising initiative that had worked for the IIHF Junior World Championships to hold the Kentucky Three-Day Event horse trials. The organizer had originally announced in February that the event, which had also been cancelled in 2020, would be cancelled for another year because holding it without paying spectators would be financially impossible. A core group of enthusiasts responded by launching an online fundraising campaign and raising $750,000. This success enabled the horse trials show category to remain viable despite the cancellation of other prestigious competitions in the category in 2021. The Badminton Horse Trials, Burwarton Show, and Burghley Horse Trials planned for the UK all ultimately decided to wait until 2022 to start again.

Other key equestrian events found ways to continue with the support of online betting sponsors and revenues, which, like many online enterprises, fared relatively well in the environment of "stay-at-home" advisories. In the United States, that growth was phenomenal and a true game changer for many sports organizations struggling to survive with little or no income from spectators. The American Gaming Association's Commercial Gaming Revenue Tracker reported that revenue from sports betting grew 230 percent in the first 10 months of 2021 compared to the same period in 2020 to reach $3.16 billion. In 2021, online sports betting in the United States generated more revenues than all the spectator tickets sold by both MLB and MLS in the United States and Canada in the 2019 season. The year 2021 also saw robust growth in online betting in Europe of 19 percent over 2020.

Sports betting supported the first traditional horse race series on the 2021 international event calendar, the Cheltenham Festival, March 17 to 19, in England, which was under very tight lockdown restrictions at the time. The event also demonstrated how COVID protocols could work safely on outdoor courses in this sport. The Grand National also took place without spectators in April. Jockeys and horse owners shared some of the burdens of racing without ticket revenues as the prize money was reduced by about 25 percent.

By May, major equestrian events were able to accommodate limited numbers of spectators. The Kentucky Derby took place on its traditional date, the first Saturday in May. The number of spectators on site was 30 percent of capacity, which had been 165,000 in 2019. While some observers expressed concern that COVID-19 infections could spread at the race, only a dozen spectators tested positive for COVID-19 afterward, and none experienced serious illness. The second race in the prestigious "Triple Crown"—the Preakness Stakes—took place on May 15, with 15,000 spectators in attendance.

The third race in the "Triple Crown" series, the Belmont Stakes, allowed spectators with conditions that became a standard practice as more sports welcomed back spectators. All ticket holders had to show proof of complete COVID-19 vaccination or a negative test for COVID-19 completed in the past 24 hours. Spectator attendance was capped at 11,000, just 10 percent of historical attendance.

The financial reports of the operator of the Belmont Stakes, the New York Racing Association (NYRA), showed how equestrian sports learned to adapt to pandemic restrictions while maintaining a healthy financial outlook. NYRA conducted all races in the 2020 season without spectators at the three tracks it operates: Aqueduct Racetrack, Belmont Park, and Saratoga Racecourse. The average revenue per race day increased substantially—by 19 percent—over 2019. The fast growth of online betting more than made up for the loss of revenues from ticket and concession sales.

The other sport that benefitted substantially from growth in online betting, international football, had to adapt to high player salaries and additional costs for COVID-19 prevention measures. Payroll's share of total revenues exceeded 70 percent at top tier clubs. But additional income from sports betting sponsorships helped to offset losses in spectator revenues. Thanks to increased sponsorship and advertising revenues from sports betting, total revenue declines were small and managed through expense control at top tier football clubs.

The long-term outlook for top tier international football clubs was better. Using recent transactions from the 2021 season, Forbes analysts estimated that the top 20 football franchises increased in value by 30 percent in the previous two years. FC Barcelona and Real Madrid topped the list at over $4.7 billion each; the average valuation of the top 20 teams was $2.28 billion. Large increases in the use of digital media during the pandemic and sports betting revenues supported financial strength. After central banks dropped interest rates to stimulate economic recovery, businesses that generated dependable revenues through broadcast contracts became even more valuable.

Test and Trace

Sports event organizers cautiously welcomed back spectators with events officially organized as test events. This engaged health industry experts to evaluate the COVID-19 prevention strategies and facilitated the development of long-term plans to "live with the virus" while making spectator attendance possible.

The UEFA 2020 Men's Championship was postponed a year to 2021. UEFA had the strong advantages of excellent financial resources and the ability to retain over 500 experienced employees to continue working on preparations. UEFA has maintained a policy of keeping 500 million euros in reserves before making contributions to sports charities.

The four Euro 2020 matches planned for Wembley Stadium near London were officially designated test events for the UK's Events Research Program (ERP). The semifinals and final matches in July were authorized to hold 60,000 spectators, or 75 percent of Wembley's usual capacity. All spectators needed to present proof of full vaccination at least 14 days earlier or a current negative PCR test. Nonetheless, Public Health Scotland reported that 1,991 spectators who had attended one of the four Euro 2020 matches at Wembley or three matches in Glasgow had developed COVID-19 infections in the week following their visit to the stadium; the exposure could have occurred traveling to the match or celebrating elsewhere afterward, but the timing of the infections pointed to an elevated risk of infection.

The Euro 2020 final at Wembley on July 11 was recognized as a worst-case scenario "Superspreader" event. Public Health England said

2,295 individuals were likely to have been infectious, with a further 3,404 potentially acquiring infection nearby, based on contact-tracing data. The infection rate of 8.5 percent was 54 times higher than the national average of 0.16 percent during the same period and 1,700 times higher than in Germany at that time.

Other results from the Events Research Program evaluations showed that there was evidence of COVID-19 transmission at large sports events, but that the levels of transmission were comparable to or lower than local conditions at the same time. The British Formula One Grand Prix at Silverstone in July attracted 350,000 spectators over three days. According to national "Test and Trace" reports, 585 cases and zero fatalities were associated with the race. Only 242 were considered likely to have been acquired by attendees at the event, an infection rate less than 0.07 percent. The Wimbledon tennis classic, with just over 300,000 spectators attending two weeks of matches, reported 881 cases to "Test and Trace."

Steps to minimize the risk of COVID-19 transmission among spectators at Wimbledon 2021 were an integral part of the test event strategy. Fully vaccinated ticket holders from the UK whose last vaccination was at least two weeks earlier could complete entry with confirmation by a standardized mobile phone app. All other spectators had to show proof of a negative COVID-19 lateral flow test within the previous 48 hours.

The range of COVID-19 precautions used at the 12 other venues for the Euro 2020 matches provided a different type of test by observing and contrasting different approaches in different facilities. Budapest authorized full capacity, Copenhagen 70 percent, St. Petersburg 50 percent, and Munich just 20 percent. The Munich matches used automated contact-tracing through mandatory registration with the "Corona Warn App." UEFA required host cities to guarantee at least 20 percent of stadium capacity attendance and moved matches from Bilbao, Spain, to Seville after Bilbao health authorities declined the demand. It became obvious to television audiences that guidelines on social distancing were not being followed by fans clustered closely together in stadiums and cheering. UEFA's policy projected weakness. The fine print on tickets and web links indicated that volunteers would notify spectators of noncompliance and reserved the right to remove offenders, but no visible action was taken.

Tests of COVID-19 precautions at Euro 2020 matches were informative but often showed weaknesses. As a result, health agencies were more inclined to limit or prohibit spectator attendance at sports events when larger regional outbreaks occurred later in 2021.

The downside risk of full sports stadiums was illuminated again by a contact-tracing report from the Wisconsin Department of Public Health. This showed that spectators at spring 2021 Milwaukee Bucks basketball games and celebrations experienced 659 confirmed COVID-19 cases and probably caused 133 secondary infections. This did not present decision makers with any easy choices. Images of fans cheering in packed sports stadiums had been used extensively in public awareness campaigns to encourage vaccination and follow rules during lockdown periods. Taking away this incentive could potentially cause more harm than good.

The Pause Button

Top tier sports organizations determined to finish their 2020–2021 seasons, but COVID-19 outbreaks occurred regularly and required even more determination to manage and then move on. Headline-grabbing cases of outbreaks showed that even the best managed and best funded top performers could not achieve their goals without COVID-19 disruptions:

- In October 2020, the Tennessee Titans became the first NFL team to report over 20 COVID-19 infections among players and staff, prompting a series of postponements.
- In November, the Rugby Autumn Nations Cup cancelled its opening match when five players from the Fiji national team tested positive and teammates designated close contacts had to isolate.
- In December, English Premiership Rugby cancelled two matches and a championship when multiple players tested positive for COVID-19.
- In December, the English Premier League postponed the Tottenham versus Fulham match after the visiting team had already arrived at the stadium because a series of COVID-19 cases made Fulham unable to compete; outbreaks at three other teams caused six additional postponements.

- In December, the English Football League had to postpone a total of eight matches after teams reported extensive COVID-19 outbreaks that made them unable to field enough players.
- On New Year's Day, Ohio State announced that 16 players could not play in the Sugar Bowl, not specifically citing COVID-19 but not noting any other reason. This followed an earlier outbreak that affected 17 players and 3 assistant coaches in December. Sugar Bowl opponent Clemson reported an even larger outbreak, taking 37 of the 120 men on the football team out of competition. These large outbreaks mirrored disruptions across college sports teams.
- In January 2021, in just one week, a total of five NBA teams reported COVID-19 outbreaks—the Wizards, 76ers, Heat, Celtics, and Mavericks; the Philadelphia 76ers could only field the minimum requirement of eight players for one game.
- In February, France's National Rugby Team had an outbreak infecting 11 players, resulting in a series of postponements in World Rugby's Six Nations Cup.
- In March, MLS franchise Inter Miami CF cancelled three scheduled preseason matches following an outbreak at its team.
- In May, the Indian Premier League suspended the 2021 season after three players tested positive for COVID-19.
- In May, the New York Yankees reported a COVID-19 outbreak infecting nine vaccinated players and four staff members.
- In June, the Phoenix Suns isolated a single COVID-19 breakthrough infection by mandating quarantines until two consecutive negative test results were obtained; NBA All-Star Chris Paul was forced to miss two games.
- In July, the Milwaukee Bucks were challenged in the NBA finals by six COVID-19 infections among medical and support staff and one player, Thanasis Antetokounmpo. Antetokounmpo's brother, Giannis, was not isolated as a close contact and continued to play.
- In July, the Colorado Department of Public Health classified the MLB All-Star game at Coors Field as a COVID-19 outbreak, with 14 cases contracted at the event.

- In September, the Boston Red Sox were hit hard by a COVID-19 outbreak that infected 12 players at one time.
- In October, the MLB mandated full vaccination for the Baseball World Series, but the General Manager of the winning Atlanta Braves team Alex Anthopoulos and Jason Castro of the Houston Astros had to isolate after positive COVID-19 tests.

The Fight Continues

A "light at the end of the tunnel" was not in sight as 2021 neared an end. Austria was in complete lockdown; the Netherlands mandated that professional sports take place with no spectators present behind closed doors and then went into a complete lockdown as well. Germany tried out spectator attendance limits with additional strict vaccination and same-day COVID test documents for stadium access, but ultimately mandated that professional sports take place with no spectators behind closed doors. The World University Winter Games, planned for Lucerne, Switzerland, in December 2020 and then postponed until December 2021, were cancelled two weeks before the scheduled start. Switzerland's hospitals had run out of capacity to treat serious sports injuries, and quarantine requirements made it more difficult for athletes to travel.

The UK, which had ended almost all COVID-19 related restrictions on July 17, 2021, saw new COVID infection figures reach record highs. Then, the United States reported more than 2 million infections in one week and a record daily figure of 430,000. France, Italy, Switzerland, Denmark, Portugal, Greece, and Australia also reported daily records of new COVID infections. The Australian state of Victoria reported that 4 percent of the entire population was infected with COVID at the end of 2021, although 90 percent of the adults were vaccinated.

Data from France showed new variants and waning effectiveness of vaccinations over time were increasing COVID-19 infections. At the end of 2021, about 0.65 percent of adults who had been fully vaccinated less than six months earlier were found to have new COVID-19 infections each day. That rate was half the rate for unvaccinated adults, but it was about 400 times higher than the COVID-19 infection rate for vaccinated adults during the previous summer. This higher rate of "breakthrough infections" matched an acceleration of COVID-19 infections at sports teams.

The NBA, which reported that 97 percent of players had been fully vaccinated and 65 percent had received booster shots, still had to postpone nine December matches because some teams could not activate a total of eight players after COVID-19 infections or exposures depleted rosters. The Boston Bruins were short by seven players and the Cleveland Cavaliers by eight. By the end of December, two-thirds of the 450 active players in the NBA had contracted a COVID-19 infection. The NBA's leadership determined to carry out the full season and continue to postpone matches as necessary. This became one more case where sports leaders ultimately concluded that COVID-19 infections would not be eliminated in the near future, and contingency planning would need to continue as the global health crisis continued.

COVID-19 outbreaks wreaked havoc with the schedules and finances of professional sports leagues. In mid-December, the number of COVID-19 infections reported among players and staff in a one-week period reached a record high in the English Premier League, at 42. Half of the league's matches scheduled for the weekend before Christmas were postponed. The matches that did take place had to find replacements for players inactivated because of COVID-19 infections or exposure. The Liverpool Reds had to close their high-performance training center after both the team's assistant manager and head coach tested positive for COVID-19.

At Christmas, 5 of the 13 teams in Switzerland's Ice Hockey National League were in quarantine and unable to compete. The NHL had to postpone a record 91 games in the autumn of 2021 because of COVID-19 related player unavailability. As a result, the NHL decided not to release players to compete in the 2022 Winter Olympics and use this two-week period to reschedule the 2021 postponements.

The NFL had even more challenges. The league set a new record in 2021, but it was not good news. The autumn game between the Pittsburgh Steelers and Baltimore Ravens was rescheduled a record four times until both teams could activate enough players to complete a roster. Originally set for November 25, the game was moved to November 28, then November 30, and then December 1. It ultimately took place on December 5, and an action-packed match rewarded fans for the wait. The Pittsburgh Steelers clinched a victory with a final score of 20–19.

In the following week, the NFL set another record. Forty-seven players tested positive for COVID-19, bringing the total of players on the COVID-19 reserve list and unavailable to play to 126. Extensive vaccination of 95 percent of all players in the league limited the health risks, but that did not eliminate them. Two-thirds of the players infected had no symptoms, and the other third was reported to have only mild symptoms and ultimately cleared their infections without hospitalization. The high level of COVID-19 infections caused three more games to be postponed. Ultimately, the NFL and its players' association decided to reduce the mandatory isolation period for asymptomatic players and staff from 10 days to 5 days, contingent upon negative COVID-19 test results.

Around the world, COVID-19 infections impacting players and mandatory quarantines continued to steadily disrupt sports schedules. The case of Los Angeles Lakers star LeBron James illustrated the complexity of evaluating the risks for vaccinated players. After James had a positive test result, he was inactivated for two days, until he produced two negative test results on two consecutive days. Football player Kevin Mbabu of the Swiss National Team and German Bundesliga, who had already recovered from COVID-19 in the summer of 2020, contracted a new breakthrough infection and had to quarantine for two weeks in Dubai before returning home. At the IIHF World Juniors Hockey championship, the U.S. national team had to forfeit a game to Switzerland when the entire team was required to quarantine following player positive test results. Paris St. Germain football star Lionel Messi and four of his teammates tested positive for COVID-19 and had to miss the French Cup match.

Just when it seemed that things could not get worse, they did. Most of the tennis players who competed in the Mubadala World Tennis Championship in Abu Dhabi in December 2021 tested positive for COVID-19 on arrival or shortly afterward. The first was U.S. Open champion Emma Raducanu. The Olympic gold medalist, Belinda Bencic, followed. Ons Jabeur, who replaced Raducanu and defeated Bencic in the women's match, tested positive and went into quarantine afterward. Rafael Nadal and his coach, Carlos Moya, as well as assistant coach Marc Lopez, became cases four through six. Then, players Denis Shapovalov and Andrey Rublev reported positive COVID-19 tests. Andy Murray, who had recovered from COVID-19 a year earlier and subsequently received both vaccinations and a booster shot, was the only original player at the competition who did NOT report a COVID-19 infection afterward. All infected players reported having completed full vaccination, just like 97 percent of the players registered for the ATP World Tour tennis series. At the same time in mid-December, tennis champions Benoit Paire, Aslan Karatsev, and Evgeny Donskoy, as well as Men's Tennis World Number One—Novak Djokovic—were confronted with positive COVID-19 tests.

Djokovic's positive COVID-19 test set off a firestorm of negative publicity. He had been a vocal opponent of vaccination, was not vaccinated at all against COVID-19, and had already been infected with the virus in June 2020 after disregarding COVID-19 prevention recommendations. He subsequently confessed to proceeding with an interview in person with a French journalist, while the player knew he was infected and had no excuse for not switching the format to a video interview. Djokovic ultimately lost his effort to secure a visa for Australia to compete in the 2022 Australian Open and was publicly chastised by the government as a danger to public health.

Benoit Paire's candor about the toll that two years of COVID-19 precautions and infections had taken showed that "living with the virus" might be possible for athletes, but it would not be easy. Paire had already had COVID-19 infections at the U.S. Open and Hamburg Open in 2020 and was confronting his third infection, a triple breakthrough infection, after completing full vaccination. He told his followers on Twitter, "I have had enough of this COVID chaos. Because of COVID I have an infection in my nose, but because of all these quarantines in hotel rooms around the world, I feel sick in my head." Paire underscored his message with a photo of his cramped quarantine hotel room and his fast-food restaurant delivery on New Year's Eve.

Cumulative experience managing COVID-19 issues showed that there were seven distinct reasons why high-performance athletes were more vulnerable to COVID-19 exposure and infections than other individuals of their age and health:

- The superior physical fitness of top athletes made most of this group's COVID-19 infections asymptomatic. Eighty-two percent of the professional athletes who tested positive for COVID-19 in 2021 displayed no symptoms. They were

nonetheless infectious and capable of transmitting the infection to others.
- Athletes competing at away games or international competitions have greater exposure to "hotspots" than individuals who remain in one location and take additional precautions when larger regional outbreaks occur. Research published by the Wall Street Journal showed that local transmission of COVID-19 reached peaks in different regions at different times, strongly influenced by the amount of time people spent indoors during specific seasons.
- Elite athletes have come to depend on support from large numbers of specialists to optimize performance, ranging from chauffeurs and helicopter pilots to physiotherapists and professional chefs. Most professional athletes earning over $1 million a year are required by their insurance companies to have a bodyguard when they are in public places. Every NHL team has a team dentist at practices and games. In Olympic sports, there are an average of seven such support specialists for each athlete. The Olympic Channel featured this in a series called "Gold Medal Entourage." Some functions, such as nutritional guidance, could be performed remotely, but most require in-person contacts.
- Financial penalties used to enforce COVID-19 prevention policies that had at least some influence on the general public were insignificant to top earning athletes. The NFL fined Aaron Rodgers $14,000 for violating COVID-19 protocols. That amount equals three months of income for the average American, but just four hours of Rodgers' $33 million annual compensation from the Green Bay Packers and just one-hundredth of one percent of the quarterback's total assets.
- Routine and frequent activities that are typical for athletes in most competitive sports are classified as high risk to very high risk by medical experts for respiratory infections in general and COVID-19 in particular—traveling by plane, eating at a buffet, working out at a gym, giving ceremonial handshakes, and simply playing contact sports.

- Long-distance international travel emerged as particularly risky for athletes who needed to fly frequently to accumulate points on competition circuits. Forty-two percent of the athletes who flew to Australia to compete at the 2021 Australian Open were exposed to another passenger who tested positive for COVID-19 on arrival in Australia, although all passengers presented current negative COVID-19 tests or proof of recovery in the past three months before boarding the flights. Two of the athletes themselves tested positive afterward.
- Elite athletic competition has very high rates of injuries requiring in-person medical treatment and physical rehabilitation. Most of the athletes competing in the FIS Ski World Cup are injured at least once during each season. Athletes have a much higher risk of contracting COVID-19 infections during their medical treatment and rehabilitation than patients who can switch to telemedicine for their treatments.

The 2022 FIFA World Cup test matches in Qatar in December 2021 showed a glimpse of what might be possible in the future. Crowds cheered the opening at an open-air stadium in a celebratory atmosphere with a spectacular nighttime show and with conditions. International guests had to be vaccinated and still had to complete a two-day quarantine and test negative again before seeing Doha and the FIFA matches. Faced with player shortages due to COVID-19, one team forfeited its place, and Algeria substituted junior players from its development team. The story had a happy ending. The junior players from Algeria rose to the challenge and won the championship for their country.

A Case in Point: The ATP World Tour

The traditional image of elite athletes is that they try their best and never quit. The reality in professional tennis is that lower ranked players do not earn enough to cover the travel and training expenses required to compete internationally and cannot work in a conventional salaried position while they travel on the ATP World Tour. This entire pool of talent faced financial ruin and forced retirement from professional tennis when the season was suspended in March 2020 because of the global COVID-19 pandemic.

The ATP World Tour resumed on August 14, 2020, but 45 tournaments scheduled in 2020 and 2021 were cancelled due to COVID-19 prohibitions on large events or international travel restrictions. Tournaments that relied more heavily on spectator ticket sales to cover costs and distribute prize money were especially hard hit by pandemic restrictions. In 2019, the nine ATP 1000 Masters tournaments—the most prestigious after the four "Grand Slams"—derived 45 percent of their revenues from ticket sales and purchases by spectators. On average, sponsorships contributed 27 percent of revenues and broadcast rights just 23 percent. Smaller tournaments depended even more on revenues from ticket sales and purchases by spectators, which contributed over 70 percent of their total budgets.

ATP management cut operating costs by 23 percent but needed to plan for double-digit increases in insurance premiums in the future. Tournament revenue declines rippled through prize money payouts. In 2021, prize money declined 7 percent from 2019 at the ATP Next-Gen Finals. Prize money declined an unprecedented 60 percent from 2019 at the 2021 Miami Open.

Before the pandemic struck, 87 percent of professional tennis players earned less than $100,000 a year in prize money. Most earned less than $20,000 a year in prize money. Prestigious tournaments also paid tens of thousands of dollars to higher ranked players at invitational events to ensure the quality of competition and promote ticket sales. When the season was suspended for five months, players had no opportunities to earn prize money. And rising stars had no opportunities to earn ranking points to gain invitations to tournaments that paid participation fees in addition to prize money.

ATP leaders and top-ranked tennis players recognized the importance of retaining the talent of the lower ranked players, who were essential for completing tournament rosters and keeping the tournament circuit lively and relevant to more fans. They put extra effort into finding solutions to give lower ranked players the opportunities they needed to invest in their tennis careers. The first part of the solution was to get the top 12 ranked players to agree to a reduction in their bonus pool. This made about $5 million available for support payments to lower ranked players.

The second part of the solution was to adjust the points ranking system so that players who missed opportunities to compete due to cancellations and postponements would not be at a disadvantage. ATP also set aside funds to pay for the costs of players who were quarantined following a positive COVID-19 test.

The solidarity support for lower ranked players helped to achieve the important goal of retaining talent in the sport. But it did not change the ongoing challenge that tournament operators, who have historically been nonprofit community organizations, have few financial resources to invest in the sport's future. ATP observed that the lower tier of ATP 250 tournaments did not make profits before the pandemic. While tennis maintained excellent prestige and ranked in the top five sports for global television audience reach during the pandemic period, the average decline in player compensation of 40 percent was one of the largest declines in all professional sports. This clouded prospects for a return to prepandemic levels of activity and marked a step backward for inclusiveness in sports.

After research in 2020 showed that only a very small fraction of COVID-19 transmissions occurred outdoors, fitness facilities in many countries began their restart programs with outdoor alternatives.

Photo by Max Donner in Murten, Switzerland, April 3, 2021.

Key Sources and References

Australian Associated Press. January 31, 2021. "Tennis Tour Hardship Looms beyond Australian Open, says Lleyton Hewitt." *The Guardian*.

Beaton, A. September 6, 2021. "Why Vaccines Are Competitive Advantages for NFL Teams in 2021." *The Wall Street Journal*.

Cohen, B. December 1, 2021. "LeBron James Out Indefinitely Under NBA's Covid Protocols." *The Wall Street Journal*.

Dedaj, P. December 21, 2021. "NBA Commissioner Adam Silver Says League Has 'No Plans' to Pause Season Amid Rise in COVID Cases." Fox News.com.

Jurejko, J. February 8, 2021. "Australian Open: Fans Back as Grand Slam Gets Under Way in Melbourne." *BBC.com*.

McKenna, P. "NYRA Registers all-Sources Handle of More Than $1.8 billion for 2020." *NYRA Bets Newsletter*. www.nyra.com/aqueduct/news/nyra-registers-all-sources-handle-of-more-than-$1.8-billion-for-2020.

Owen D. October 11, 2021. "ISU Strikes Blow for Transparency by Disclosing $2 Million Insurance Payout." Insidethegames.biz.

Reuters News staff. August 20, 2021. "Euro 2020 Final at Wembley was a 'Superspreader' Event." Reuters.com. www.reuters.com/lifestyle/sports/soccer-euro-2020-final-wembley-was-superspreader-event-times-2021-08-20/.

Stone, S. December 15, 2021, "Manchester United Report More Positive Cases in Covid-19 Outbreak." BBC.com.

Weber, J. June 29, 2021, "How High is the Risk of Contracting COVID-19 in a stadium?" *Deutsche Welle*. www.dw.com/en/fact-check-how-high-is-the-risk-of-contracting-covid-19-in-a-stadium/a-58092284.

CHAPTER 4

Health Perspectives

Strength for Health

The sports world provides the rest of the world with many inspiring examples of spectacular recoveries from life-threatening injuries to regain top condition and become a champion. Surfer Owen Wright's recovery after a devastating wipeout in 2015 is the kind of comeback many long for to put the worst of the COVID-19 pandemic behind us. At the 2015 World Surfing League championship, Wright fell from a 15-foot wave, which swept his body through the ocean and left him unconscious with serious injuries. The brain injuries made him unable to walk or exercise, let alone surf again. But he persevered with a demanding physical rehabilitation regimen and focused on his long-term goals of peak performance. Just two years later, he achieved victory as champion of the World Surfing League Quicksilver Pro Gold Coast competition. His winning streak continued. Wright went on to win a bronze medal at the Summer Olympics in 2021.

This inspirational comeback is one of many. At the 2016 Summer Olympics, Dutch road cycling racer Annemiek van Vleuten was injured with a concussion and three cracks in her spine when she crashed during a race. One year later, she won the UCI world championship title in the same event and won again in 2018. She went on to win a gold medal in the race at the Tokyo 2020 Summer Olympics.

Athletics champion and 2016 Olympian Alexi Pappas observed ways that athletic training can significantly strengthen recovery from serious health challenges in a July 2021 audio interview on *The Olympic Channel*. Pappas noted that athletes view injuries as normal, and they also know to seek help, be patient, and then see the injuries heal. They also have tools to recognize warning signs of injuries and illness that help them access treatment and adapt.

The resilience many athletes have demonstrated when challenged by serious and sometimes life-threatening injuries is based on more than athletic strength. Exercise and physical fitness build a foundation for better recoveries from health challenges, a foundation whose value has been highlighted by outcomes observed in the COVID-19 pandemic.

- The Cardiovascular Research Institute of the University of Virginia found that regular cardiovascular exercise for 30 minutes a day prevented or substantially reduced the risk of acute respiratory disease. This condition affected over two-thirds of American COVID-19 patients whose symptoms were so severe that they needed to be admitted to intensive care. This exercise regimen alone would not prevent infection from an exposure to COVID-19 but would substantially reduce the risk of it becoming a life-threatening illness.
- Researchers at the University of Bristol consolidated 30 studies which collectively showed that chronic illnesses that regular exercise can often prevent were associated with a substantially higher risk of hospitalization or death in patients infected with the COVID-19 virus. The cases studied in 2020 showed that diabetes more than doubled the risk of death in patients infected with COVID-19 and that the risk of death for younger patients with diabetes was even higher—more than three times the risk for other COVID-19 patients in the same age group.
- A French study showed that the severity of disease and risk of death increased with the level of obesity in COVID-19 patients. The study also reported that those with a Body Mass Index over 35 (severely obese) required mechanical ventilators in intensive care seven times more often than COVID-19 patients in a normal weight range. These observations were consistent with the very high COVID-19 death toll in the United States, where 75 percent of the adult population was classified as overweight, obese, or severely obese.
- A June 2021 study by Public Health Scotland published in "*The Lancet*" showed that while vaccination substantially reduced the risk of infection with COVID-19, the risk of severe illness and hospitalization was much higher for vaccinated individuals with five or more comorbidities, such as obesity,

diabetes, or breast cancer. Regular exercise has been shown to be effective in preventing many of these comorbidity factors.
- In August 2021, the *Wall Street Journal* summarized findings from multiple U.S. hospitals that also showed that the incidence of COVID-19 hospitalization was as much as 96.6 percent lower for COVID-19 vaccine recipients than for unvaccinated individuals; almost all vaccinated U.S. patients who were hospitalized had chronic health problems, and many of these could have been avoided with regular exercise. The U.S. Center for Disease Control and Prevention (CDC) reinforced these findings with a notice that adults of any age are at increased risk of severe illness from COVID-19 if they are diagnosed with heart disease, Type 2 diabetes, or obesity.
- A study of 1,700 athletes published in the *International Journal of Cardiovascular Sciences* showed that the rates of severe illness and hospitalization among athletes infected with COVID-19 were much lower than for nonathletes in their age groups.

Rigorous exercise regimens and athletic conditioning did not protect thousands of athletes from being infected with COVID-19. The first reported cases in the NBA showed how challenging this would be. When the first two COVID-19 infections in the league were reported at the Utah Jazz in March 2020, it showed how a typical league schedule of matchups could result in all 30 teams in the league having had direct contact with Utah Jazz players or a team who had played against the Utah Jazz in the previous two weeks.

When a group of top-ranked tennis players and support staff became infected with COVID-19 at a single event in June 2020, the sports world got a powerful reminder of how quickly the virus could spread and how disruptive this could be. The "Adria Tour" was initially positioned as a postlockdown restart effort to recreate the atmosphere of a prepandemic tournament with fans in attendance and cheerful camaraderie among the tennis players. World number one Novak Djokovic helped to organize and promote the tournament. In the last week of June, four players—Grigor Dimitrov, Borna Coric, Viktor Troicki, and Djokovic himself—tested positive for COVID-19. In addition, Dimitrov's personal trainer

Kristijan Groh, Djokovic's physiotherapist Marko Paniki, and Djokovic's wife Jelena all tested positive for COVID-19. The infections occurred at the same time as an outbreak of five COVID-19 cases in the local Belgrade "Red Star" football club, which underscored the vulnerability of team sports to COVID-19 transmission.

There was no sophisticated contact tracing system in place at the tournament, and the players sent out Twitter notifications regarding their test results advising everyone they had been in contact with to get tested for COVID-19. That response, combined with event photos that showed little regard for the formal health protocols of the affiliated sports associations, unleashed a wave of bad publicity. The leading French daily "Le Figaro" went as far as to call the event a "fiasco." Nonetheless, the organizers managed to control the damage sufficiently to get sponsorship and funding to hold the event again in 2021, although with no spectators in attendance.

On July 2, ten days after the initial positive test results, Djokovic and his wife reported negative test results showing they were no longer infected. Then both were free to resume their schedules. Grigor Dimitrov, however, had a prolonged struggle with his infection. Dimitrov was diagnosed with "Long COVID," an outcome of a COVID-19 infection in which symptoms such as loss of taste and fatigue continue for months after the initial infection with COVID-19 is no longer present in tests. Dimitrov tried competing in the U.S. Open in September 2020, but he lost in the second round.

Novak Djokovic had many obstacles to overcome. A COVID-19 infection, the 10-day self-isolation period it mandated, and the related burdens of managing staff, sponsors, and fan communications tested his ability to maintain his standing as the world's top ranked male tennis player. He went on to achieve victories at all nine ATP Masters 1000 championships in the 2020 season and set a new world record for the highest total number of weeks ranked as the number one player in men's tennis. He capped these achievements by winning the 2021 Wimbledon Men's Singles Tennis title, just one year after his COVID-19 infection put competition and training on hold.

The experience of Olympic tennis champion Andy Murray in contracting COVID-19 highlighted the additional challenges athletes faced in accessing the best training for optimal performance. The 2012 and

2016 Olympic Men's Singles gold medalist had to give up professional tennis in January 2019 after hip injuries made it too painful for him to continue competing. Just five months later, after rigorous physical therapy and innovative surgery, Murray resumed his professional career and won a doubles title. Murray slowly but steadily progressed toward the top tier of international tennis players and welcomed the opportunity to compete at the first Grand Slam tournament of 2021. A COVID-19 infection dashed Andy Murray's hopes.

On January 14, 2021, Murray reported a positive COVID-19 test just two days before he was scheduled to fly to Australia and start the mandatory two-week quarantine required of all international players and staff at the Australian Open. While the Australian Open did not start until February 8 and Murray recovered from COVID-19 symptoms in time to compete at the ATP Biella Challenger in Italy on February 7, he did not have sufficient time to complete the mandatory two-week quarantine to qualify for the Australian Open. Murray's victory in his semifinal match at the Biella Challenger on February 13 confirmed his physical fitness to compete in elite tennis tournaments. However, the high risks of transmission and severe illness related to COVID-19 made the rigid precautions of the Australian Open tournament organizers a wise choice.

Andy Murray was convinced that he contracted the COVID-19 infection at the All England Lawn Tennis Association's elite training center in Roehampton in early January 2021. He based his conclusion on the circumstance that his only other contacts during that period had been with family members who all tested negative at the same time. Tennis player Dan Evans shared Murray's assessment of COVID-19 spread at the Roehampton training facility during this period. The frequency of testing did not screen out all infections, and there was an outbreak involving several tennis players and staff; at peak times, both the indoor tennis courts and exercise facilities were at full capacity, and not all the tennis players there followed social distancing guidelines all the time.

The specific timing of Murray's COVID-19 infection spotlighted a particular health challenge for top athletes. The international sports calendar is arranged years in advance, qualifying for competitions is a lengthy and demanding task, and the need to customize a training program for the schedule of a competition is critical for success. Rescheduling of events on an unprecedented level and temporary closures and capacity limitations at training facilities made this even more difficult. At the same time, health care systems that were designed for peak periods were stretched beyond limits when COVID-19 pandemic peaks occurred. January 2021 was an extreme peak in Great Britain, and strict lockdown measures that included closing gyms and private indoor tennis clubs left Murray with almost no other alternative to train. While some other athletes traveled to Dubai for outdoor winter training there, a few also contracted COVID-19 infections either while traveling or during their stay.

Novak Djokovic and Andy Murray were just two of many elite athletes who contracted COVID-19. Usain Bolt, winner of eight Olympic gold medals, Cristiano Ronaldo, five-time winner of the FIFA Ballon d'Or, Lewis Hamilton, winner of seven Formula One Racing world championship titles, five-time NFL Most Valuable Player Tom Brady, Jack Nicklaus— the winner of the most PGA Majors golf championships, and hundreds of other top performing sports legends all experienced COVID-19 infections and had to adapt their careers. There has been a modest benefit from this misfortune. Because elite athletes train at the upper limits of their capacities, researchers in the field of human performance have gained additional insights that benefit the general public.

New research by MIT, the Texas Medical Association, and the Technical University of Berlin enabled better management of COVID-19 risks related to athletic training and other activities. These studies were neither encouraging nor inspirational, but they showed that workable solutions for fitness training and most sports could be implemented.

- MIT mathematics experts Martin Bazant and John Bush conducted an extensive analysis of indoor facilities to model the relative risk of COVID-19 infections. They included evaluations of various sports facilities and shared key findings in an open-access app and website to support case-specific calculations. The research showed that physical distance between persons is only one of several factors in indoor transmission. The number of individuals present, the size of the facility, airflow, and time spent in the facility also influence the risk of exposure to an airborne virus.

Transmission rates impacted by mutation characteristics and vaccination status are also key factors. Using this scientific approach, changing an exercise routine from one hour twice a week at a full gym to six days a week for 20 minutes at a gym with a maximum of three persons present emerged as a workable solution. The European fitness franchise "Body Hit" has provided this alternative to its members. The research also makes it easier to schedule support activities for physical fitness, such as physiotherapy and optimized meal plans.

- The Texas Medical Association compared a wide range of activities and measured the relative risk of a COVID-19 infection. The comparison used working for one week in an average office building as the intermediate point for "moderate risk." Swimming in a public pool was rated with the same intermediate risk, but select sports activities were found to have a much lower risk, specifically playing tennis outdoors and playing golf. Ice skating outdoors was classified as a moderate risk, slightly lower than attending an outdoor sports event. By comparison, team sports such as football and basketball were observed to have higher risks of COVID-19 infection, and working out at a gym was classified as high risk.

- In 2020, the Technical University of Berlin applied expert knowledge of air flow dynamics used to optimize laboratory "clean rooms" and public buildings to study the transmission of COVID-19 at different facilities used for different functions. The study found that the much higher rates and intensities of exhalation at indoor fitness facilities caused a much higher risk of COVID-19 infection compared to a facility like an auditorium, where attendees were stationary and breathing normally. The technical studies also showed that there were specific steps for refreshing the quantity of fresh air with no contaminants and filtering air using equipment such as that used by hospitals to substantially reduce the quantity of infectious particles. The research team consolidated these findings in a web-based app, which they made available to the public in November 2020.

Consolidating the knowledge gained from university studies has enabled some health care experts to determine constructive approaches to substantially reducing the risk of contracting COVID-19 while exercising. In an advice column published by CNET, infectious disease expert Dr. Sandra Kesh shared these recommendations for reducing the risk of exercising at a gym from medium risk to low risk: exercising with enforced capacity limits or at off-peak times of day, maintaining greater distances from others exercising, seeking out facilities that are well ventilated with well maintained air filters, and wearing a mask while exercising. While wearing a mask might seem suboptimal for sports performance, specialized exercise regimens simulate high-altitude training by systematically reducing the amount of oxygen in each breath; fit bodies can adapt to this. Sports nutrition regimens can adapt to lower oxygen intake with mineral supplements.

While research progress has helped much of the sports world resume activities during the pandemic, it has also shown that there are no simple solutions. Test events for spectator sports organized during Phase 3 of Great Britain's easing of COVID-19 related restrictions showed how some large facilities could accommodate large numbers of spectators without a measurably elevated risk of coronavirus infection. But studies also showed that air travel demonstrated one of the highest risks of COVID-19 infection. This is a significant risk for spectators traveling to see sports events and a much greater risk for athletes who must travel to multiple competitions with rigid schedules. There were dozens of cases of athletes who presented negative COVID-19 test results before boarding a flight and then tested positive upon arrival. In many cases, other athletes traveling on the same carriers had to self-isolate for 5 to 14 days even if they tested negative for COVID-19. These self-isolation experiences disrupted training regimens and deprived athletes competing in point-based series like the ATP World Tour or PGA Tour of irreplaceable opportunities to accumulate points toward their goals.

Learning Experiences

While COVID-19 infections hit the sports industry particularly hard, traditional sports organization practices for maintaining excellent physical condition and monitoring by health care professionals enabled many athletes infected with COVID-19 to overcome the disease and resume their careers. There was not a single fatality from COVID-19 reported among the over 6,600 athletes who had already qualified to compete in the Tokyo Summer Olympics before qualifications were suspended in March 2020 to accommodate the event's one-year postponement. Different athletes drew upon different training and different perspectives to overcome COVID-19 and recover, but they all had one thing in common—they never quit.

These lessons are important for other communities because of the way that asymptomatic COVID-19 cases cause transmission. When the COVID-19 outbreak began in 2020, the U.S. Center for Disease Control published a model forecasting that the entire population of the United States would be exposed to COVID-19 at some point in the future. German forecasters estimated that over half of the country's population would become infected at some point. France crossed that threshold in 2022. Understanding how many athletes have developed ways to maintain their health and overcome COVID infections will be a valuable addition to the knowledge needed for the world economy to function while a dangerous virus continues to circulate.

A good example of the way the sports industry was able to contribute to health experts' knowledge of risk management was the practices selected for COVID-19 testing frequency. These could not eliminate COVID-19 from the athlete population, but select cases showed that they could prevent community transmission. The Tokyo Summer Olympics and the 2021 Australian Open both found COVID-19 positives through rigorous testing. At the Summer Olympics, 29 positive tests among the 10,305 athletes accredited resulted in self-isolation. At the Australian Open, the ratio of positives to the total tested was one percent. In both cases, it was possible to isolate the positives and their contacts in time to prevent community transmission. It was not easy, but it was possible.

Sports also provided a learning laboratory for so-called "breakthrough" cases of COVID-19 in fully vaccinated individuals. While medical experts were impressed with the high effectiveness of the first vaccines widely used to reduce COVID-19 transmission, none was 100 percent effective in blocking transmission. Most sports, involving frequent travel and high numbers of personal contacts, presented a higher risk. And the numbers bore this out. Six members of the San Diego Padres baseball team tested positive for COVID-19 after the entire team had been fully vaccinated. The University of Mississippi football team adopted a policy of vaccinating all athletes and staff. Nonetheless, head coach Lane Griffin tested positive for COVID-19 and was isolated with mild symptoms at the start of the 2021–2022 season. Over the course of the season, "breakthrough" cases of COVID-19 among vaccinated athletes became common and resulted in hundreds of substitutions and postponements.

Analysis of sports team data demonstrated that available vaccines could reduce severe illness but could not eliminate widespread outbreaks in a vaccinated team. The NHL Ottawa Senators had a 100 percent vaccination rate but experienced two large outbreaks. The first, in November 2021, sidelined 10 of the 24 players and the assistant coach. The following month, nine additional players and another coach became infected, bringing the share of breakthrough infections to 80 percent.

Leading sports organizations became a valuable resource for health care professionals. Extensive testing of athletes with well-documented health histories helped to understand the high incidence of asymptomatic cases and the dynamics of asymptomatic infections. The NBA worked together with researchers to analyze how long players could remain infectious and what isolation practices were the safest. The results showed that 10 days was the maximum period required for self-isolation following an asymptomatic infection to minimize the risk of infecting other contacts. This standard was widely adopted by employers and schools afterward.

The NFL integrated infection test results with contact tracing data to produce leading-edge research about COVID-19 infection risks. The results were adopted by the U.S. Center for Disease Control and other health agencies. The information showed that 15 minutes of cumulative exposure to a COVID-19 infected individual was as likely to cause a new infection as a single 15 minute contact and that the common 6 foot social distancing guideline should be adjusted for ventilation and the type of activity taking place.

The *Journal of the American Medical Association* published a study of nearly 800 athletes who had tested positive for COVID-19 to evaluate health risks that could emerge after infections. Bluetooth-connected contact tracing apps provided detailed data to evaluate the comparative risks of routine activities in spreading infections. This did not reward sports with a golden image since results showed that playing team sports indoors without a medical mask was an activity highly likely to spread infections.

COVID recovery cases from the sports world have been encouraging and have shared insights for the challenge of living with the virus. Because athletes must have physical examinations and health testing more frequently and more rigorously than almost any other profession, the data provided to medical experts evaluating COVID-19 infections has been valuable and—in some cases—irreplaceable.

The sports industry has also shown that any business dependent on working in teams with frequent interaction required to achieve goals has an elevated risk of infections spreading. The sports industry likewise showed how professions that require frequent long-distance travel and interacting with local support staff in multiple locations also face increased risk of exposure. Almost half of the players in the NBA tested positive for COVID-19 before the end of the 2020–2021 season. Every team in Formula 1 racing experienced COVID-19 infections at some point. Teams that have managed this risk and sports events that have overcome the challenges are showing ways that other organizations can also keep calm and carry on. And recurring waves of COVID-19 infections in many countries are making demonstrated success in managing COVID-19 risks in workplaces essential for maintaining the confidence of clients and investors.

Recoveries and Resilience

As the number of COVID-19 infections among high-performance athletes climbed into the thousands, the sports industry learned that there were a wide range of outcomes. Sports professionals helped the health care industry observe important differences and incorporate this knowledge into strategies for recovery. One of the earliest examples was the comparative experience of cyclist Fernando Gaviria and golfer Jack Nicklaus.

Gaviria and Nicklaus were the first two world champion athletes to fight a serious case of COVID-19 in the winter of 2020. Gavira, a 25-year-old from Columbia who competed with Team Emirates, was hospitalized for 18 days. He was then in isolation for an additional 10 days to reach recovery and get clearance to train and travel again. Nicklaus, who was 80 years old at the time, began a self-quarantine at home with his wife on March 12 and tested positive for coronavirus shortly afterward. The isolation period continued for nearly six weeks, followed by a negative COVID-19 test, but Nicklaus found his personal experience with the illness "short-lived and relatively minor."

Gaviria made headlines when he tested positive for COVID-19 again in October 2020 during the Giro d'Italia. He had already completed 16 stages of the race, which required rigorous COVID-19 testing, and he had also raced in competition for 40 days in the previous four months. Gaviria outpaced the world's top cyclists to win stages in three international races held in July, August, and September. In 2020, the second positive case was a rarity. Only 25 cases of reinfection had been confirmed in the first nine months of 2020. But even diseases for which reinfection is rare, such as chicken pox, have reported instances of second infections. Soon afterward, reinfection cases rose sharply, and sports leaders had to develop plans to minimize the impact on competition and accelerate recoveries.

These two early cases provided an important reminder that the strength of athletic conditioning can benefit recovery from a disease so serious that it caused over five million deaths in two years, but athletic strength alone does not prevent infection. The comparison also showed that younger athletes could not take a speedy recovery for granted. Policy makers trying to prepare treatment plans observed that COVID-19 deaths increased with age, but the serious cases experienced by Gaviria and other young athletes showed that other factors were important. Comorbidities such as diabetes and cancer increased the risks of serious illness and death; these factors increased with age and were reflected in the higher number of serious COVID-19 cases in older populations.

Many young athletes who became ill with symptomatic COVID-19 experienced challenges with recovery and regaining strength:

- Mohammed Bamba of the NBA Orlando Magic contracted COVID-19 in early June 2020 and was able to clear his infection before screening to enter the NBA Bubble. While he played in the NBA Bubble in July, he experienced continued muscle fatigue and soreness and did not recover sufficiently to resume his most rigorous training regimens for six months.

- Alex de Minaur, Australia's top-ranked men's tennis player, tested positive for COVID-19 ten days before the start of the Summer Olympics and had to withdraw. His training program had been designed to peak at the Olympics and after a relatively long recovery period, he had to redesign his training regimen to regain his form over a six-month period.
- Asia Durr of the WNBA New York Liberty was diagnosed with long-haul COVID, a condition that persists for months after the infection is cleared and the patient is no longer contagious. She had chronic fatigue and breathing difficulties, and was unable to play for an entire season.
- Justin Foster, an NCAA team football star, was also diagnosed with long-haul COVID, which aggravated the asthma conditions he already had; Foster had difficulty just breathing and walking, so a return to exercise and sports became impossible.
- Yoán Moncada of the MLB Chicago White Sox had symptomatic COVID-19 in July 2020 and had to miss training camp. He played after clearing his infection, but his performance declined measurably from the previous season, with his hitting average dropping from .315 to .225.
- Tommy Sweeny of the NFL Buffalo Bills developed myocarditis, a heart ailment, after clearing a COVID-19 infection and was unable to play for the entire following season. Four other athletes of the 790 reported COVID-19 cases in North American pro sports during 2020 also developed heart inflammation conditions that kept them inactive for the next season. This was a disappointment, but medical experts noted that the incidence of cardiac complications following a COVID-19 infection for professional athletes was about half the level found in the general population, a positive sign for the benefits of regular exercise.
- Jayson Tatum of the NBA Boston Celtics contracted COVID-19 in January 2021 and was cleared to play again after two weeks. He reported intermittent lapses of breathing difficulties that kept him from playing at 100 percent.

- Emma Raducanu, the 2021 U.S. Open Women's tennis champion, contracted COVID-19 in December 2021 and recovered slowly. She noted that she had to substantially reduce the time and intensity of her workouts to avoid risking injury by resuming training at her previous level.

Adapting training and conditioning for recovery after COVID-19 quarantines and illnesses became a key component of sports organizations' efforts to "live with the virus." Research published in the medical journal "*Chest*" in August 2021 showed that individuals who had recovered from COVID-19 had a 45 percent lower aerobic capacity after their recovery, which reduced their capacity for exercise or high-performance sports. A common risk was hyperventilating during rigorous exercise.

Acknowledging that a quick return to prior training levels increased the risk of injury, revised training programs emphasized gradual steps. The first step was a thorough physical exam to be certain that no organs or tissues had been damaged too severely to constrain physical activity. A standard program was to start with running and moderate weight lifting and increase the performance goals by 20 percent after preinfection performance levels were reached. Stanford Health Care experts recommended taking three to four weeks to gradually return to previous activity levels.

The athletes diagnosed with long-haul COVID faced bigger challenges to adapt their athletic training and return to sports at their previous level, let alone take it to the next level. Approximately 10 percent of England's Olympic and Paralympic athletes had COVID-19 conditions such as fatigue lasting more than 30 days and were unable to resume training for months.

New Challenges for Fitness

Exercise and fitness played an important role in reducing the severity of many cases of COVID-19 infection. The seismic shift of restructuring traditional office jobs to "work from home" positions increased the importance of maintaining employee health in remote locations and added a set of new challenges for employers. Surveys of German health insurance providers and large employers polled by FitTech of Munich highlighted increased back pain claims from "work from home" employees as well as sick leave linked to the disruptiveness and screen fatigue of remote work routines. U.S. health insurance companies reported that emergency room admissions for injuries caused by exercise at home rose 42 percent in the first year of the pandemic.

Fitness industry specialists have been able to offer additional solutions such as remote health and fitness monitoring and packages of online exercise programs that make it easier to try out fitness regimens that restore an employee's stamina and can strengthen immune systems. But the way that the pandemic disrupted the choices for staying healthy and achieving fitness goals made health maintenance especially challenging.

The COVID-19 pandemic disrupted every aspect of the fitness industry but also spurred creative approaches that can enable long-term expansion. Even in Sweden, which had fewer lockdowns and curfews to stem the spread of COVID-19 infections, gyms were required to limit the number of users based on their size. Singapore, which was ranked first in the Bloomberg COVID Resilience survey, closed indoor fitness facilities completely during its circuit breaker lockdown from April to June 2020. It did this once again when restrictions were introduced for four weeks in May 2021 to enable the city-state's vaccination program to gain momentum. Most countries required indoor gyms to close entirely during "hard lockdown" periods, and many insisted on rigorous hygiene standards as a condition for approval to reopen.

There is no question that making indoor gyms adapt their operations to the elevated health risks of the COVID-19 pandemic was an essential policy to combat the unchecked spread of COVID-19 infections. The risk that COVID-19 infections which had spread in gyms could further strain health care providers made this critical. Multiple health agencies around the world, which used sophisticated contact tracing programs, reported serious outbreaks of COVID-19 related to infections spread at indoor gyms:

- In September 2020, the Chicago Public Health Department reported that 68 percent of the members of a single gym who attended classes the week of August 24 had either tested positive for COVID-19 infections or been treated for symptoms. While the gym had been required to limit attendance to 25 percent of its maximum capacity and direct members to exercise at least six feet apart from other members, these precautions were ineffective against the highly infectious COVID-19 virus.

- In October 2020, a report by the Canadian Broadcasting Corporation showed how COVID-19 infections at one fitness studio, Spinco of Hamilton, Ontario, caused over 100 documented COVID-19 infections. Of these, 48 were found in members and staff of the studio, 15 were infected in households with members, 30 at schools and workplaces, and 6 at health care facilities where the primary infections were diagnosed and treated.
- In January 2021, Malaysian authorities closed nine gyms that had been identified as the source of COVID-19 clusters.
- In March 2021, the Hong Kong Free Press reported that a COVID-19 infected fitness trainer at Ursus Fitness had spread the infection to 7 staff and 10 members; at least 32 secondary infections were associated with individuals who had been infected at the gym, which public health authorities closed.
- In April 2021, Radio Canada reported that 440 infections had been linked to Mega Gym 24 in Quebec City: 190 of these were primary infections of members or staff, and 250 were associated with workplaces at which infected Mega Gym members had been present. One month later, an additional 260 COVID-19 infections and 12 deaths were traced to the outbreak.

While fitness industry professional associations often cited surveys showing that gyms posed relatively lower risks of COVID-19 infections than some other business locations, none of these studies could claim that the risk of infection was insignificant. A study by researchers from Stanford and Northwestern Universities published in the journal *"Nature"* offered a very different perspective. An analysis of anonymized cell phone data and changes in movement following postlockdown reopenings in the summer of 2020 found that indoor fitness facilities accounted for the second highest incidence of new COVID-19 infections in the United States, surpassed only by restaurants.

A later study in Germany in autumn 2021 showed that rigorous hygiene measures at sports facilities could substantially reduce, but not eliminate, risk of COVID-19 transmission in sports and exercise facilities. Data from Germany's "Luca" contact tracing app showed that only 0.8 percent of users testing positive for COVID-19 had been exposed at a gym or sports club. This measure excluded swimming pools, which accounted for an additional 0.6 percent of reported exposures.

Large, well-publicized, and frequent COVID-19 outbreaks spread at indoor fitness facilities destroyed alliances with the health insurance industry that had taken decades to build. A study by the Blue Cross/Blue Shield health insurance organization showed that insurers' average costs for severe COVID-19 infections requiring hospitalization were $45,000. This figure reached $100,000 when intensive care and mechanical ventilation were required. These costs far exceeded the savings insurers had achieved when their clients modestly reduced health care costs by working out regularly, often encouraged by health insurance discounts.

A 2021 survey conducted by Nautilus forecast that 12 percent to 30 percent of individuals who had previously purchased a fitness club membership would never again subscribe to a gym. The financial pressure was too much for many establishments, and about a quarter of the gyms in the United States closed permanently. Three of the largest international fitness facility networks filed for bankruptcy: Gold's Gym, Town Sports International, and 24 Hour Fitness.

The financial pressure of COVID-19 precautions was massive for ClassPass, which had been the sports business star of 2019 and achieved a billion-dollar valuation that year. The Class Pass business model emphasized negotiated group discounts for guest use of fitness facilities and building a valuable database of members' fitness interests. This could not accommodate frequent, abrupt closures of fitness facilities or capacity restrictions that limited access to full-time members only. In April 2020, the company announced that it would eliminate 22 percent of staff positions and furlough an additional 31 percent of the employees.

The risk of COVID-19 infections at indoor fitness clubs and frequent government mandated restrictions and closures spurred phenomenal growth in the outdoor fitness and at-home fitness industries. This was reflected in real user data reported by Strava, a fitness app that tracks users' specific fitness activities and duration. Outdoor fitness increased greatly in countries that made exceptions for individual exercise outdoors during lockdowns: 28 percent in the United States, 45 percent in Germany, and 82 percent in the UK.

The cycling industry reported robust growth following the start of the COVID-19 pandemic. In the United States, sales of mountain bikes increased at an annual rate of 116 percent, and the urban & fitness bike category grew 126 percent year over year following the COVID-19 pandemic. In the UK, the Bicycle Association reported 45 percent growth in bicycle sales from January 2020 to January 2021, despite significant sales missed due to inventory shortages.

The spectacular growth in recreational cycling did not rescue organizations and events for professional cycling competitors. USA Cycling cut 15 percent of its staff positions permanently and furloughed 25 percent of the remaining staff to balance its budget after clinics, races, and other events needed to be cancelled to comply with public health restrictions. British Cycling furloughed 90 workers. The International Cycling Union (UCI) announced full or partial furloughs for all 130 staff members in 2020 and closed its state-of-the-art training facility for elite athletes. UCI explained that 650 cycling events that had been scheduled for 2020 had been cancelled or postponed, resulting in a corresponding loss of sponsorship and ticketing revenue.

Participation in golf increased significantly and reversed a decade long decline. Golf benefited from being an outdoor sport that had always incorporated distance between players as part of its form. Golf was exempted from lockdown restrictions in most locations, although precautions to restrict close contacts in social facilities or tournaments were often implemented to minimize the risk of COVID infections. The results were good. No outbreaks were reported at golf clubs that followed local health rules.

In the United States, the number of new golf players reached an all-time high record in 2020, at 6.2 million. The total number of completed rounds of golf played in 2020 increased by 14 percent to surpass 500 million. In Germany, which licenses golf players, the number of licenses increased by 1.4 percent and industry revenues grew by 5 percent in 2020, despite a two-month mandatory closure of golf courses in the spring. Globally, the number of new golf players reached an all-time record in 2020.

The golf industry did not experience the financial pressures that downsized the leadership organizations in cycling. A focus on clubs financed by member dues and green fees, and tournament organizers who managed to reschedule rather than cancel almost all planned events, maintained a stable financial foundation.

The boom in home-based fitness training and equipment was unprecedented. While sports equipment suppliers had to be exceptionally nimble, in many categories sales more than doubled. Previously, most sports equipment sales had been to large organizations like fitness clubs, which were financed by monthly dues payments. The sudden shift to home-based business supported the sale of high-ticket items, plus future potential to cross-sell and upsell accessories to a much larger installed base.

The share price movements of TechnoGym reflected investor confidence that the momentum of the home fitness equipment industry would continue. Unlike major consumer products companies, whose shares merely declined when pandemic related lockdowns were introduced widely in March 2020, TechnoGym's shares crashed. The company, which reported 85 percent of total revenues in 2019 from the manufacturing and service of exercise equipment for health clubs and teams of professional athletes, saw its market value of 500 million euros cut in half in just one month. A year later, the company's market value had rebounded to January 2020 levels, based on the phenomenal growth of TechnoGym's at-home fitness equipment sales. Year-over-year growth in home equipment sales was 50 percent in the first half of 2020. The company remained profitable throughout the pandemic, and total profits for the first half of 2021 matched pre-pandemic levels of 2019. Maintaining profit levels with home fitness sales is allowing the company to maintain its ambitious research and development program. The steady stream of new world records achieved by athletes who trained with the latest TechnoGym equipment demonstrated that the latest product improvements had measurable benefits.

A Case in Point: Megatlon Fitness Clubs

The COVID-19 pandemic forced three of the world's largest international fitness club organizations to declare bankruptcy, and many fitness clubs closed permanently. In Buenos Aires, Argentina, 15 percent of the 1,350 fitness clubs open at the start of 2020 had closed by the end of the year. At the same time, the Megatlon Network of fitness clubs adapted quickly to the pandemic to continue growing and finding new opportunities to expand within Argentina and abroad.

The focus of Megatlon's response to the COVID-19 pandemic was a hybrid model that created a wide choice of at-home and outdoor fitness options and complemented the physical facilities when they were permitted to reopen. After Buenos Aires began a four-month lockdown on March 19, 2020, Megatlon management quickly launched a new webcast offering called "Megatlon At Home" on Instagram. The classes began attracting 10,000 participants a day, and the Megatlon following on Instagram grew from 30,000 to 200,000 in six months. Online spinning classes used the Zoom platform to recreate the vibe of a high-energy spinning class for members in their home or garage. While Megatlon's 51 fitness clubs were located in Argentina's three largest cities, the online following grew throughout Argentina and Latin America. Fifty of the clubs reopened in December 2020 with new health measures implemented.

The large social media following enabled Megatlon to gain new subscribers for its new fitness app, available on iOS, Android, and Windows devices. This supported cross-selling and upselling more profitable services. Megatlon featured "Virtual Trainer" classes with 200 dedicated instructors; this also helped Megatlon retain the expertise and client relationships of its coaching staff and avoid layoffs. Megatlon also expanded into the market for home gyms, offering members both preselected packages of workout accessories to use at home and a members-only online shop with exclusive discounts for custom solutions. This approach leveraged Megatlon's purchasing power as the largest fitness network in Argentina to obtain lower prices for its members. It also secured lower prices for its own expansion into the outdoor gym market.

Megatlon's new outdoor exercise product line used courtyards and parking lots at five gyms in its existing network. It also operated outdoor fitness classes at a half-dozen public parks and organized an outdoor running club plus an outdoor cycling club to build on the growing interest in outdoor fitness activities. For rainy days, the network introduced an innovative program for the pandemic era called "Flash Training." This gave members the option of achieving key fitness goals in 20-minute compact workouts so that no contact was over 10 minutes. This followed scientific findings about reducing COVID-19 infection risk by reducing the time of potential exposure.

Megatlon reengineered its core business of fitness clubs and classes to reduce COVID-19 infection risks and make members feel as safe as possible as the pandemic continued in a series of waves. It engaged the clinic of an infectious disease expert, Dr. Daniel Stamboulian, to develop a specific set of practices for this new challenge. The key elements were:

- Securing a COVID-19 health clearance from the health department for each club before reopening
- Limiting maximum attendance to 30 percent of capacity
- Temperature checks at check-in
- Separation of all exercise equipment by a minimum of two meters
- Maximum utilization of 50 percent of equipment, leaving 50 percent remaining available for disinfection by the hygiene team
- Upgraded ventilation systems increasing the circulation of fresh air from outdoors
- Mandatory reservations at a set time and location in staggered shifts to avoid the need for queues

The 30 percent capacity limit required members to reserve their workout in advance online. This provided Megatlon with accurate contact tracing information to prevent any outbreaks at its gyms. The reservation details were saved as a single QR code to scan at check-in so that social distancing could be maintained at gym entrances.

Megatlon marketing employed the 30 percent capacity limitation as a sales tool. New memberships and reactivations of expired memberships were offered in blocks of 50. No new memberships were available for weeks at a time, so that the company had leeway to gradually increase prices to help cover the costs of COVID-19 prevention measures. The price increase policy was subtle; a 40 percent discount was offered at reopening and the discount was reduced every two months to 15 percent at the end of 2021. The new capacity limit policy also became an incentive to retain memberships rather than take a chance that no memberships would be available after trying out another gym or home workout program. Since the historic client turnover rate had been 30 percent and the sales costs of acquiring new members to replace them were often equal to six months of member fees, the reduced cancellation rate strengthened Megatlon's profits. Megatlon also expanded its services to corporate clients and developed exercise solutions for the physical strains of working from home.

By adapting its business practices to the challenges of the pandemic, Megatlon was able to retain its most valuable asset, its trained staff of 1,500. Continued growth allowed the team to grow to 1,600 by the end of 2021. The network's founder and CEO, Fernando Storchi, described adaptation to the pandemic in an autumn 2020 interview with "Presenterse" magazine: "We see growth. Evolution and innovation are constant factors. We are going to end up reinventing ourselves as a company."

The sports business industry responded to the health challenges posed by waves of COVID-19 infections with technologies that support better health and fitness, together with marketing programs to highlight approaches to train safely.

Photo by Max Donner at FIBO, Cologne, Germany April 8, 2022.

Key Sources and References

AFP News Agency. June 23, 2020. "Djokovic et trois joueurs positifs au Coronavirus: Comment l'exhibition a tourné au fiasco sanitaire." *F Sport*.

Barney, J. April 15, 2020. "Exercise May Protect Against Deadly Covid-19 Complication, Research Suggests." *UVA Today Newsletter*. https://news.virginia.edu/content/exercise-may-protect-against-deadly-covid-19-complication-research-suggests.

Branswell, H. June 25, 2020, "CDC Broadens Guidance on Americans Facing Risk of Severe Covid-19." *StatNews*. www.statnews.com/2020/06/25/cdc-broadens-guidance-on-americans-facing-risk-of-severe-covid-19.

Carayol, T. February 6, 2021. "Andy Murray Pinpoints Lack of Vigilance at Roehampton for Catching Covid." *The Observer*.

Chandler, D. April 15, 2021. "A Method to Assess Covid-19 Transmission Risks in Indoor Settings." *MIT News*. https://news.mit.edu/2021/covid-19-risks-indoor-0415.Cohen, B. March 10, 2021. "Scientists Needed Help Against Covid-19. They Asked Sports." *The Wall Street Journal*.

Doolittle, D. July 7, 2020. "What's More Risky, Going to a Bar or Opening the Mail?" *Texas Medical Association Newsletter*.

Evans, M. August 28, 2021. "U.S. Covid-19 Hospitalizations Approach a Peak as Delta Variant Spreads." *The Wall Street Journal*.

Kast, B. August 19, 2021. "Many of Michigan's Biggest Insurance Companies Will No Longer Waive COVID-19 Costs." WXYZNews.com.

Kriegel, M. November 17, 2020. "Coronavirus: Web App Calculates Potential Risk of Infection via Aerosol Particles." TU Berlin Press Release.

Livingston, M. July 24, 2021. "10 Activities That Expose you to Coronavirus, From Most to Least Risky." CNET.com.

Ohlson, E., A. Monnoyeur, and E. Ohlson. April 25, 2021. "The Fitness Market—United States."

Salis, R., D.R. Young, S.Y. Tartof, J.F. Sallis, J. Sall, Q. Li, G.N. Smith, and D.A. Cohen. August 1, 2021. "Physical Inactivity Is Associated With a Higher Risk for Severe COVID-19 Outcomes: A Study in 48 440 Adult Patients." *British Journal of Sports Medicine*. https://bjsm.bmj.com/content/bjsports/early/2021/04/07/bjsports-2021-104080.full.pdf.

CHAPTER 5

The Sports Economics Challenge

Investors Pitch In

For decades, sports business had moved in just one direction—up. The industry had grown twice as fast as the world economy and did not slow down during the global economic declines of 2001 and 2008. Steadily rising payments for sports content helped, and more sophisticated pricing programs increased revenues for events. Initially, the pandemic struck the foundations of this success story with widespread cancellations and a near total loss of spectator revenues. Even top-performing organizations reported large losses—the 30 teams in Major League Baseball lost a total of $1.8 billion in 2020, compared to the $1.5 billion profit reported the year before. Investors were quick to recognize long-term opportunities and amassed unprecedented pools of funds to acquire stakes in some of the most promising sports businesses. This boosted leading sports businesses but left smaller competitors behind.

The success of American private equity investment firm Silver Lake in crafting an approach to invest in the commercial business of New Zealand's All Blacks Rugby organization showed how new strategies could get sports businesses the money they needed to grow while retaining the talent they also needed to grow. The All Blacks, like many sports clubs, had traditionally operated as a not-for-profit and used surplus revenues to support athlete development and community sports programs. The organization's goal of keeping New Zealand's best players in New Zealand faced steady competition from professional leagues in larger countries with larger budgets to attract talented players overseas.

Just one year of COVID-19 related restrictions and cancellations depleted New Zealand Rugby's finances and put its future existence in doubt. And because New Zealand had been able to largely avoid widespread outbreaks of COVID-19 by closing its borders and offering more opportunities to have sports events with spectators, the losses made it look even more difficult for sports clubs in other countries to survive beyond the pandemic. In 2020, New Zealand Rugby's financial reserves declined by 40 percent and ended the year at just NZ$ 51.8 million (approximately US$ 37 million). The first year of the pandemic had worsened an already difficult financial position following a loss of NZ$ 17 million (US$ 11 million) in 2019. The outlook for New Zealand Rugby to continue to operate at its current scale for more than two years was poor, which put New Zealand's plans to host the Women's Rugby World Cup in doubt. By traditional financial measures, its total enterprise value was headed toward zero.

New Zealand Rugby's leaders saw past these daunting challenges and promoted an optimistic perspective they called "a once in a generation opportunity to look at all areas of our business and make real change." The organization began a dialogue with Silver Lake investors in May 2020 and began exploring ways to get enough outside capital while continuing to promote the community goals that were most important to its mission. In ordinary times, raising any investment at all for a not-for-profit that had lost half of its financial reserves in two years would be very difficult and carry a high interest rate. However, the final deal reached in February 2022 set a market valuation of NZ$ 3.5 billion (US$ 2.4 billion). The transaction valued New Zealand Rugby's future revenue potential at the same level as that of the MLB's New York Mets baseball team. Innovations in the transaction showed how many other struggling sports clubs could recover from COVID-19 challenges and grow again in the future.

Five elements of the transaction showed how it could be possible to go from losing money to a multibillion dollar future.

- The commercial rights to sponsorships, media assets, licensing, and traditional spectator revenues were put together as a separate business for private investors to own partially.
- Private investors would only be allowed to own a minority interest and not acquire management control.
- New Zealand investors would be allowed to acquire some shares on similar terms, preserving community ties important to the organization.

- Players' associations would share future profits, helping to motivate performance and retain talent in New Zealand.
- The public–private partnership would be designed to develop commercial opportunities outside New Zealand and achieve greater scale.

Two years of public debate about converting a traditional not-for-profit association to a public–private partnership highlighted the ways that sports organizations could adapt. This took place very publicly because of the All Blacks' status as a national icon in New Zealand, and this paralleled a new openness to private financing that could secure a good future for many sports clubs beyond the pandemic. Many major sports organizations moved forward with ways to add more financial resources to their growth strategies.

Increased options for financing growth and strong investor interest enabled the top tier of sports businesses to contain losses from pandemic postponements, cancellations, and empty stadiums. Based on transactions that took place in the 2020–2021 period, Forbes estimated that the average team in MLB increased 3 percent in value and the increase for NFL franchises reached 14 percent. The growth in NFL team values was strengthened by record-setting fees for television rights over the next decade, estimated at a total of $110 million.

Despite pandemic challenges and empty stadiums, Fenway Sports Group received an optimistic bid valued at about UKL 3 billion to acquire the 2020 Premier League champions, the Liverpool Reds. The bid reported in April 2021 was ten times the UKL 300 million investment that Fenway Sports Group had made to acquire the team in 2010. Although the offer was politely declined, it valued the investment in the team with a 25 percent annual rate of return over the past decade. This high valuation a year after the start of the COVID-19 pandemic showed that championship sports teams stood out as quality investments that were nearly recession proof and pandemic proof.

While the NFL continued to require that team owners qualify as private investors screened and approved by the NFL as traditional team owners, other leading sports leagues found ways to accommodate professional investors whose main goal was achieving a good return on their investment. Their selection criteria sought out "patient money" with deep pockets that could hold ownership shares through the long period of recovery expected after most team operations had adapted to pandemic challenges. Key innovations earned attention:

- Spain's La Liga securitized the net income from media rights over a very long period. The first transaction was for 50 years and transferred an 8.25 percent share in the rights to CVC Capital Partners for the almost astonishing sum of 2 billion euros. This single transaction effectively made up for pandemic related losses and restored the financial means to continue operating at prepandemic levels. Germany's Bundesliga began evaluating this type of financing, but it did not move ahead immediately.
- World Rugby gained a new investment of nearly $500 million by offering 14.3 percent of the future net income of the World Rugby Six Nations Tournament to CVC partners. This single transaction *tripled* the financial assets in World Rugby's financial reserves and provided complete confidence to national rugby associations and tournament host cities that World Rugby could meet all financial obligations for the rest of the decade. The capital injection also buffered the reported loss of UKL 46 million (about US$ 62 million) for the 2020 reporting period.
- The FIVB International Volleyball League also took a major step in securing its financial future by tapping private equity. Its agreement with CVC Capital Partners restructured its activities to support the ongoing promotion of amateur volleyball and education programs by the not-for-profit organization of the FIVB while creating a new business entity for the FIVB's commercial and professional sports operations. FIVB stands to gain $100 million to $300 million from the new strategy.
- The FIBA International Basketball League established a separate business for international championship events and other competitions with profit potential. It sold a stake in the new business to an American private equity firm, GCBH LP.

The additional funding helped FIBA cover losses resulting from the pandemic period and the delay in its share of commercial revenues from the postponed 2020 Summer Olympics.
- The NBA approved more options for private investors to acquire minority ownership shares in NBA teams as financial investments with no management control starting in 2021. Five of the 30 teams in the league announced new deals soon after the new policy was finalized: the Sacramento Kings, Golden State Warriors, San Antonio Spurs, Atlanta Hawks, and Phoenix Suns.
- Major League Soccer initiated a rule change that made it easier for financial investors to own shares of teams. InterMiami's lead owner, soccer star David Beckham, gained the backing of the Ares Capital investment group with a new $150 million investment. The agreement included interest payments to Ares Capital as well as an ownership share.
- The National Hockey League introduced new policies for investments from financial funds in December 2021. This opened the door to substantial new investments for the Tampa Bay Lightning, Minnesota Wild, and Pittsburgh Penguins.

In total, sports businesses raised over five billion dollars in new investment funds from professional investor groups during 2021. The infusion of new capital did more than rescue sports clubs from the kind of financial downward spiral that had threatened the existence of many. The agreements emphasized contributions of expertise and media industry connections that could grow total revenues in the future—a classic win-win situation.

Slim Down to Shape Up

As sports organizations sought ways to remain viable for a long-term future and retain the talent that was their most valuable asset, they looked for activities they could eliminate or modify to reduce budget pressures. Success in these efforts would help retain the foundation of fans and broadcast partners that were essential for financial success.

Large financial losses caused by the pandemic accumulated quickly and required major changes to overcome. The Manchester United football club reported losses of UKL 28 million (over $40 million) for just the first 15 days of the suspended 2020 season. Europe's top 20 football clubs earned a combined €8.2 billion in 2019/2020, down 12 percent from €9.3 billion during the prior season. Estimated losses for the NFL's 2020 season reached $4 billion.

The use of cloud-based IT technologies to produce live sports broadcasts at remote facilities had begun before the pandemic. The savings in travel and time were substantial, and this approach also reduced the need for expensive temporary broadcast studios. The pandemic related social distancing guidelines and event size limits made this approach an absolute necessity in many cases. After Formula 1 racing restarted with much larger on-site broadcast teams than most other professional sports and experienced high COVID-19 infection rates, the move to remote broadcast production accelerated. The cost savings became a bonus.

These kinds of cost savings became very important for sports broadcasters confronted with entirely new business challenges during the COVID-19 pandemic. First, outright cancellation of events obliged refunds or other compensation for advertisers who signed up in advance and extra efforts to secure programming for the same time slot. Second, shortened seasons and postponements led to scheduling conflicts that were normally minimized through advance planning by sports leagues and broadcast partners. While live sports broadcasts performed relatively well compared to other television shows during the COVID-19 pandemic, they still faced significant declines in audiences:

- The average U.S. television audience for the 2020 MLB World Series dropped to 9.8 million from 13.9 million in 2019; in 2021, MLB baseball games averaged a 12 percent viewership decline compared to the prepandemic 2019 season.
- The average U.S. television audience for the NBA's 168 game regular season in 2020–2021 declined by 25 percent compared to the prepandemic 2018–2019 season.
- The NHL reported a more modest decline in viewership, dropping 2 percent in the 2020–2021 season.

- The NFL, which managed to play a full regular season in 2020–2021, also managed to regain audience growth after an initial decline during the pandemic. The average U.S. television audience for the league's regular season in 2020–2021 declined 7 percent from the previous season. The television audience rebounded in the 2021–2022 season with a 10 percent increase as games averaged 17.1 million viewers.

Despite the trend of declining television audiences, live sports far surpassed conventional television series in reaching large audiences. The NFL's average viewership of 17.1 million viewers was over three times higher than standard prime time drama and comedy series. The 2021 Academy of Motion Pictures' Oscars show recorded a 55 percent drop in viewership from 2020, with just over 10 million viewers.

The necessity of adjusting sports business operations to the pandemic meant that adjusting athlete compensation would also emerge as a key success factor to get through the pandemic and restore full operations afterward. The NFL salary cap decreased from \$198.2 million in 2020 to \$182.5 million in 2021. Spain's La Liga reduced the player salary cap for the 2021 season by an average of 2 percent. The 30 teams in Major League Baseball reduced total player compensation to \$4 billion in 2021, a reduction of 4 percent compared to 2019, the last season that was played with a full schedule. MLB teams slashed their total compensation by two-thirds in 2020, when the season was reduced to just 60 games. COVID-19 stimulus packages also stimulated inflation, which reached an annual rate of 4.7 percent in the United States in 2021 and exceeded 8 percent in spring 2022. This magnified the decrease in player compensation.

Salary cuts in smaller professional sports organizations with smaller total budgets were much larger. England's Rugby Football Union reduced player compensation by 25 percent from UKL 23,000 per game in the 2019–2020 season to UKL 17,250. Average compensation in Minor League Baseball dropped to just \$12,000 per player in the 2021 season.

When NBA teams tapped players from affiliates in its "G" League, they demonstrated the value of investing in player development programs and having viable backups. During the Omicron variant wave in the middle of the 2021–2022 season, this talent pool became essential for maintaining the season schedule and avoiding the cancellation of games by teams that could not otherwise field the minimum number of players to compete. At the end of December 2021, the 30 NBA teams had two dozen replacement players from the "G" League on their rosters. The "G" League players went from earning $37,000 per season to $138,000 for a 10-day replacement player contract. They also earned an opportunity to showcase their talents to NBA pros.

Pandemic replacement performances that spotlighted "G" League players in the NBA during the 2020–2021 season also created an opportunity to launch a new event and reposition the sport to continue growing. The following season introduced the first G League Next Gen Game during the 2022 All-Star Weekend in Cleveland.

Professional golf presented a notable contrast to team sports that struggled with financial losses and cost cutting. Golf's ability to restart quickly and prevent COVID-19 outbreaks became a competitive advantage. The sport emerged as a safe choice that broadcast partners and corporate sponsors could count on to take place as scheduled. This made sponsors and advertisers willing to pay premium prices so that they could execute traditional marketing campaigns on a planned schedule and coordinate with other media like direct mail campaigns, which are well suited to audiences staying at home. Golf's strong financial performance was reinforced by the retention of experienced staff and production crews. Prize money payouts in professional golf increased significantly during the pandemic:

- Player's Championship: from $12.5 million in 2019 to $20 million in 2022
- Genesis Open at the Riviera: from $7.1 million in 2019 to $12 million in 2022
- Arnold Palmer Invitational: from $9.1 million in 2019 to $12 million in 2022
- PGA Championship: from $11 million in 2019 to $12 million in 2022
- RBC Heritage: from $6.9 million in 2019 to $8 million in 2022
- American Express La Quinta: from $6.7 million in 2021 to $7.6 million in 2022

- Farmers Open at Torey Pines: from $7.1 million in 2019 to $8.4 million in 2022
- Phoenix Open: from $7.1 million in 2019 to $8.2 million in 2022
- Honda Classic from $6.8 million in 2019 to $8 million in 2022
- Sony Open: from $6.4 million in 2019 to $7.5 million in 2022
- LPGA Championship: from $3.1 million in 2019 to $5 million in 2022

The prize money offered at the AT + T Pebble Beach and Masters Championship at Augusta remained the same as before the pandemic, at high levels of $8.7 million and $11 million, respectively.

Even the highly successful PGA could not muster the resources to maintain all the elements of the golf ecosystem amidst travel restrictions, expensive testing protocols, and other burdens of the pandemic period. As these challenges rippled throughout the sports industry, programs that had helped promote industry growth ceased, some temporarily, others for the foreseeable future. Collectively, these cuts reduced the scale of the industry and made it more difficult for suppliers and service providers like sports medicine clinics to break even on their expenses. The range was wide, and the scope was global:

- The PGA managed to hold most competitions planned for professional golfers in 2020 and 2021, rescheduling when pandemic conditions made this necessary. However, traditional Pro-Am competitions with no television broadcast revenues were not economical and largely cancelled, starting with the PGA Memorial in May 2020. The Pro-Am events did make a comeback in 2022, starting with the American Express La Quinta tournament in January.
- In the NCAA's top tier Division 1, a total of 112 sports programs were initially eliminated in the 2020–2021 academic year. Of these, 35 were reactivated with furloughed staff rehired by the end of the academic year. Beyond the top tier of Division 1, at least 165 lower division college sports

programs were also eliminated. The cuts separated over 1,500 athletes affiliated with NCAA sports programs from coaching and training facilities they depended on to excel. The contraction also reduced the size of the talent pool to train promising athletes in the future.

- Major League Baseball reduced the number of official minor league affiliate teams from 160 to 120. Most of the teams that lost their affiliation continued to play in regional leagues; only seven discontinued operations.
- The World Masters Games 2021, planned for Kansai, Japan, in May 2021, was originally postponed to May 2022 to accommodate the rescheduling of the 2020 Tokyo Olympics. Later, the event was postponed indefinitely as continued restrictions on travel into Japan made it impossible to get over 10,000 athletes and support personnel to the venues arranged for the Games. In 2022, the event was eliminated from the World Masters Games calendar and the organization issued refunds of participation fees for athletes who had registered. The local host committee absorbed substantial losses and would not be able to host the next biennial competition, which is scheduled in Tampere, Finland, in 2023.

Comeback Trail

As vaccination programs and COVID-19 treatments emerged as one means to continue many operations while the virus continued to circulate, more sports programs that had been forced to pause were able to restart after a delay. This served several useful purposes for the sports industry. First and foremost, it reinforced the image of resilience that has been a key foundation of the sports brand and an attraction for sponsors and broadcast partners. Second, it provided a means to retain skilled workforces whose expertise is essential for presenting complex sports events as the international sports event calendar circulates the globe. Often referred to as "the Nomads" by sports insiders, these specialists make their sports event skills available worldwide and they also transfer valuable expertise to local employees and volunteers whom they train before moving on to the next event. Third, the ability to restore a larger part of the sports event calendar helped raise the level of "critical mass" for key suppliers to the sports industry. Ticketing programs, international sports hospitality vendors, stadium maintenance suppliers, and a wide range of other key contractors have high fixed costs and need higher volumes of events to service to stay in business. Recovery in many parts of the sports industry helped to achieve that goal and retain expertise for the rest of the industry.

Table 5.1 "March Back, March Forward" shows how most sports organizations overcame COVID-19 challenges to resume within two years, sometimes sooner with adjustments. These 16 landmark annual events were newsworthy enough to be covered in pandemic impact feature articles in the *Washington Post* and *UK Guardian* in spring 2020. Only one, the Manchester Six Day cycling race, was unable to get back on the calendar in 2022 and filed for bankruptcy. And this was not a total loss; registrations were transferred to the London Six Day cycling race.

The path back for landmark events was uneven and overshadowed by the COVID-19 pandemic. Cycling implemented testing and health protocols that generally worked, but it still had to cancel some 2020 events entirely and postpone some 2021 events to later dates because of local health regulations or prohibitions on large gatherings. Events planned for China in 2021 did not take place since the 21-day quarantine policy for incoming travelers was unfeasible for international sports. Events such as the Tokyo Marathon, which opened for registration in 2021 but was postponed to 2022, had to transfer their 2021 fees and sponsorships to 2022, missing out on key revenue for an additional year. Events that took place with capacity limits, such as the NCAA March Madness and the LA Marathon, also missed revenues important for maintaining full operations.

March 2021 events that were postponed to later in the year began to show light at the end of the tunnel. Vaccination and COVID-19 test certificates were widely available in many popular sports locations by autumn of 2021, making it possible to hold traditional events with modifications. The Tokyo Marathon and NYC Half Marathon showed how hybrid approaches and virtual races could help to maintain some revenues and keep sports organizations intact so they could resume full operations in the future.

2022 heralded a strong comeback for sports events. Six Nations Rugby, the Australian Formula 1 GP, and the start of NCAA March Madness all

106 SPORTS IN THE PANDEMIC ERA

Table 5.1 March Back, March Forward

Event	2020 Start Date	Cancelled/ Postponed	Notes	2021 Start Date	Cancelled/ Postponed	Notes	2022 Start Date	Cancelled/ Postponed	Event Changes
UCI Track Cycling	26-02-2020	NO	Berlin	20-10-2021	Postponed	France	12-10-2022	NO	France
Tokyo Marathon	01-03-2020	NO	Elite Athletes Only	17-10-2022	Cancelled	Fees valid 2022	06-03-2022	NO	Virtual hybrid
Six Nations Final	07-03-2020	Postponed	No spectators	26-03-2021	No spectators		09-03-2022	NO	1 million spectators
UCI Strade Bianche	07-03-2020	Postponed	New Date 01-08	6-03-2021	NO		05-3-2022	NO	
LA Marathon	08-03-2020	NO	Strict Hygiene	7-11-2021	Postponed	50% capacity	20-03-2022	NO	60% capacity
ATP Indian Wells	11-03-2020	Cancelled		06-10-2021	Postponed		10-03-2022	NO	
PGA Players	12-03-2020	Cancelled	Sawgrass	11-03-2021	NO	spectators ok	10-03-2022	NO	
Six Day Manchester	13-03-2020	Cancelled		None	Cancelled	bankruptcy	None	Cancelled	London substituted
World Athletics IC	13-03-2020	Cancelled	Nanjing, China	19-03-2021	Cancelled	Nanjing, China	18-03-2022	NO	Belgrade, Serbia

Australia F1GP	15-03-2020	Cancelled		19-11-2021	Postponed	10-04-2022	NO	record attendance
NYC Half Marathon	15-03-2020	Cancelled		14-03-2021	Cancelled	20-03-2022	NO	22,349 Finishers
NCAA Basketball	17-03-2020	Cancelled		18-03-2021	NO	Virtual only	15-03-2022	NO	
UCI Volta Catalunya	23-03-2020	Cancelled		22-03-2021	NO	25% capacity	21-3-2022	NO	
UCI E3 Classic	27-03-2020	Cancelled		26-03-2021	NO		25-03-2022	NO	
UCI Gent	29-03-2022	Postponed	New Date 11-10	29-03-2021	NO		27-03-2022	NO	
LPGA Rancho Mirage	31-03-2020	Postponed	New Date: 10-09	01-04-2021	NO		31-03-2022	NO	Prize money up 60%

THE SPORTS ECONOMICS CHALLENGE   107

reported new records for attendance. The NYC Half Marathon had nearly as many finishers in 2022 as in 2019, despite cancellations the two years before. While World Athletics still could not hold events in China as it followed a highly restrictive "zero-COVID" strategy, the organization was able to produce the 2022 World Athletics indoor championships in Belgrade, Serbia, and maintain momentum on its calendar. Positive trends continued as Madison Square Garden sold out its entire capacity in a few hours for the historic boxing match of Katie Taylor versus Amanda Serrano in April. An impressive 60 percent increase in the prize money for the LPGA Golf Championship reinforced optimism that positive trends would continue.

The rebound in sports attendance and the exit of some sports events from the annual calendar supported robust increases in ticket prices. In January 2020, the minimum price for a ticket to view the NFL Pro Bowl was $22 and the most expensive was $95 for fans who purchased directly from Ticketmaster. When the event resumed in 2022 after being cancelled in 2021, the minimum ticket price was $66 (a 200 percent increase) and the most expensive was $435 (a 350 percent increase). Event organizers which share financial reports with the public found that ticket prices increased an average of 14 percent in 2021.

Higher ticket prices and sellout crowds are providing a foundation for sports organizations that made it through the worst of the pandemic to rebuild their financial strength. But it will take most sports businesses years to recover from pandemic related financial losses. CAA Icon prepared detailed forecasts of the sports event industry in Los Angeles County, host of the 2028 Olympics. The outlook showed revenues recovering to prepandemic levels by 2023 or 2024, but several more years will be needed to make up the accumulated losses from pandemic cancellations and capacity restrictions.

The Sports Ecosystem Adapts

The dramatic challenges caused by the COVID-19 pandemic showed how all participants in the industry rely on services and talent that support the industry collectively. Athletes depend on sports equipment manufacturers for high-performance technology and sponsorships. Sports equipment companies depend on athletes to test their new designs and communicate their messages. Sports teams depend on real estate developers to build and maintain facilities that suit athletes and spectators. Real estate developers depend on sports teams to help cover the high financing costs of building and maintaining a stadium. In the crisis environment after the sports industry shut down when COVID-19 emerged as a global pandemic in March 2020, these connections were disrupted. As sports restarted, most of the industry found ways to adapt, but some businesses did not survive, leaving the industry transformed.

Sports industry insiders got a look at what the postpandemic future of sports would look like when FIBO, the world's largest fitness industry trade show, presented its first live exhibition since April 2019 in April 2022. The downsizing was noticeable. The 2019 show had set new records with 1,133 exhibitors in 11 pavilions and 145,000 attendees. The 2022 show was smaller than ten years earlier and featured 600 exhibitors in six pavilions, while attendance was limited to 50,000 visitors to accommodate social distancing guidelines. Attendees had to show proof of COVID-19 vaccination or recovery just to get into the show.

The adage "less is more" was on display at FIBO in 2022. Sports industry insiders could see how athletes and teams could continue setting new records by training more efficiently and more flexibly using sophisticated sports science and a wider choice of ways to achieve high performance with hybrid solutions connecting physical facilities to athletes on the go—or at home.

This collection of sports businesses that had the strength to get through the pandemic and get back on track to grow again presented a futuristic vision of how the sports industry will be able to adapt to the disruption of the COVID-19 pandemic. The organizers emphasized the capabilities of the sports and fitness industries to maintain good health, prevent infections with stronger immune systems, and accelerate recovery. Standout exhibitors showed how:

- Whoop, which had earned attention early in the pandemic for its monitor's ability to observe signs of COVID-19 infections and declines in blood oxygen levels, catapulted its dynamic growth during the pandemic into a new launch of its product line in Germany.

- Symbiont won medical certification for its sensor-equipped exercise outfits, which measure key performance and health metrics during physical exercise.
- Rubtiler, a supplier of cushioned flooring for gyms and sports facilities, featured a "Vir&Bact Protect" product line, which a certification institute showed to be at least 85 percent effective in killing human coronaviruses; the product is also at least 65 percent effective in eliminating influenza viruses.

A new sports nutrition product symbolized the energy behind the sports industry's focused rebound. Called "Beyond Resilience," its formula mixes optimal quantities of nutrients for recovery from exercise to improve results for each hour of effort. The company managed to start its operations and organize manufacturing and distribution during Austria's second lockdown in autumn 2020. After expanding to the Middle East, the company set its sights on global distribution in 2022.

The FIBO 2022 exhibitors featured key trends highlighting the dynamics of sports businesses that had maintained operations during the pandemic and were now expanding:

- Fitness equipment companies are customizing devices for home use, convenient storage, remote instruction and coaching, and performance measurement.
- The technical expertise and supply chains for manufacturing and maintaining sports equipment remained intact throughout the pandemic and were available to support future growth.
- Data-driven artificial intelligence programs are being applied to improve both athlete training and more efficient business operations.
- The infrastructure for recovery and rehabilitation facilities available to sports participants is expanding and building on increased awareness of the benefits of preventative health care.
- Hygienic products designed to combat transmission of virus and bacteria particles in sports facilities became widely available, providing another practical solution for "living with the virus."

- Scalable business solutions demonstrated that they were capable of scaling back when confronted with a major disruption to operations, such as a temporary lockdown.

The advances and sophisticated applications of technologies exhibited by standouts at FIBO in 2022 covered a very wide range. But these sports business winners also had a key success factor in common with the first tier of sports teams and leagues, which had been successful in obtaining large investments after they were struck by the COVID-19 pandemic. These firms were all *bankable*. They had established followings, strong and growing social media visibility, contracts to sustain future cash flows, endorsements by admired athletes, efficient operations, and recognized brands. The strongest performers had excellent intellectual property rights secured by patents, copyrights, and trademarks. They also demonstrated flexibility to complement their product offerings and maintain relationships with customers by introducing or expanding hybrid online and mobile services. These strengths enabled them to retain their most valuable asset, the skilled experts who contribute to their firms as employees and contractors.

Investors showed confidence that the select sports businesses that had adapted to the COVID-19 pandemic were now well positioned to grow in the future. In September 2021, eGym completed a fifth round financing with an additional $41 million investment from Mayfair Equity Partners. This brought its total valuation to over $260 million, a major increase from the $15 million the information technology company raised when it launched in 2014.

Destination Winners and Losers

For decades, cities and regions competed actively to host major sports events. Many sought to strengthen tourism promotion, while others sought to gain more benefits from large investments like convention centers and airports. The top tier of sports event competitions continued during the COVID-19 pandemic. Queensland, Australia, secured a host city contract for the 2032 Summer Olympics in July 2021, while Sapporo, Salt Lake City, and Barcelona continued promotion of their bids to host the 2030 Winter Olympics.

Most regions subordinated sports destination marketing to public health priorities once the pandemic began. And most had no choice. Travel bans made it difficult to get key talent to international sports events and capacity limits at quarantine facilities, testing facilities, and hospitals made it impractical to accommodate hundreds of athletes and serve local needs at the same time. Just a few regions had managed to redeploy resources for COVID era international sports events. This enabled them to maintain opportunities for skilled sports industry workers and secure this advantage to compete for future sports events. The notable winners were:

- Dubai and the United Arab Emirates: This Middle East travel hub was able to accommodate major international sports events that had been scheduled in other regions by putting four competitive advantages to work. First, the UAE's two flag carriers, Emirates and Etihad, maintained service on hundreds of international routes to support international cargo operations, which also offered more choices for passenger travel to the region. Second, the nearby desert made sophisticated air filtration equipment essential before the pandemic. Third, the dry, sunny climate made organizing support services and hospitality outdoors easier and more dependable. And, in 2021, the UAE was able to quickly implement a mass vaccination campaign that successfully reduced local COVID cases. The UAE accommodated Indian Premier League Cricket, the 2021 Australian Open Women's Qualifying Matches, and 2021 FIFA Women's World Cup qualifying matches when these could not be held at the originally planned locations due to pandemic restrictions.
- Florida: The Sunshine State became the pacesetter for "living with the virus" approaches to presenting sports events. Florida's quick response to enable UFC and the NBA to relocate and restart events in Florida in the spring of 2020 distinguished the state as able to accommodate sports during a global health crisis. The state's own professional sports teams found ways to welcome spectators outdoors with capacity

limits and social distancing and helped retain skilled workers. The 2021 NFL Super Bowl spotlighted Florida's capabilities.
- Mexico: Mexico's response to the COVID-19 pandemic was controversial, but it made the country available for presenting almost all summer sports events. By the end of 2021, Mexico reported 4 million COVID-19 infections and 300,000 deaths. The country remained open for international travelers without quarantine restrictions, and hotels continued to operate. From the perspective of sports event organizers, Mexico was a dependable choice. International sports enterprises produced twenty outdoor sports competitions in Mexico in 2021, including the World Surf League Corona Open Mexico, the Mexico City Grand Prix, and the WTA Finals, which were relocated on short notice from Shenzen, China. Mexico will now continue to host the WTA finals through 2030.
- Switzerland: Switzerland generally permitted outdoor sports throughout the pandemic with some size limitations so that traditional trace and quarantine procedures could limit infections and prevent community transmission. When an outbreak occurred at a ski instructor school in Wengen, it was contained, and a major ski championship planned for the area was moved successfully with modest effort. Switzerland kept its winter sports facilities open at half capacity throughout the 2020–2021 season, while most other European countries limited access to professional athletes or closed entirely. Switzerland's "COVID Pass" for fully vaccinated individuals enabled spectator sports to welcome back fans, with some attendance limits if required by local health care system needs. The shift of many winter sports events to Switzerland has given the country a competitive advantage that will last for several years.

At the other end of the spectrum, China's "zero-COVID" policy of strictly limiting inbound travel and requiring quarantines for most international arrivals resulted in mass cancellation of international sports events and raised doubts about China's availability to accommodate international sports events in the next few years. The Beijing 2022 Winter Olympics were given exceptional permission to proceed with stringent COVID-19 protocols, but test events scheduled for 2020 and 2021 were carried out with domestic Chinese participation. Initially the postponement of the World University Games to June 2022 in Chengdu, China, and the previously scheduled Hangzhou 2022 Asian Games also received special approval. But as strict pandemic controls continued in 2022, these international events were postponed to 2023. Other major events such as the Asian Beach Games, the ISU Four Continents Championships and Figure Skating finals, the IBU Biathlon World Cup, the UWW Asian Wrestling Championships, the WTA Finals, and the Shanghai Rolex Masters were ultimately cancelled. China's twelve international marathon races were postponed indefinitely.

A disastrous result at the May 2021 Ultra Marathon caused China's government to ban all "high-risk" sport competitions. Twenty-one of the 174 runners who started the race died of hypothermia on the course, which lacked preparations for the harsh weather they encountered. Chinese organizations showed little interest in competitions for future international sports events. Rebuilding a skilled workforce and facilities to welcome international sports in the future would require large investments.

A Case in Point: Rose Bowl Operating Company

The Rose Bowl in Pasadena, California, was renowned as "America's Stadium." In addition to the annual Rose Bowl NCAA football competition scheduled annually on each New Year's Day, the stadium presented home games for the UCLA college football team and other major sports events, plus large concerts and sprawling outdoor events such as fairs for antiques and collectibles. Like many large stadiums around the world, the Rose Bowl was owned by the local government, in this case, the City of Pasadena. Its charter was to operate as a not-for-profit benefiting the community. In 2019, it reported typical not-for-profit results with a surplus of just $335,000.

Rose Bowl Operating Company did not make profits to build financial reserves, and when the COVID-19 pandemic forced the cancellation of large gatherings at the stadium, the projected loss of $20 million in revenues far exceeded the $3.5 million in reserves held in its accounts for an unforeseen event such as an earthquake. While the 2021 Rose Bowl Game took place on New Year's Day as scheduled, it was moved to Dallas, Texas, to comply with local California restrictions against large gatherings during the COVID-19 pandemic. These restrictions continued until June 15, 2021.

The short-term solution for the management company, the Rose Bowl Operating Company (RBOC), was difficult and expensive. Although in the past, RBOC had operated the stadium without direct support from the City of Pasadena, the COVID-19 pandemic made it imperative to seek $11.5 million from the City of Pasadena's operating budget so that it could pay interest on the $231 million bond issued to finance renovations and improvements in the previous decade. Management anticipated that a future direct payment from the City of Pasadena of $9.3 million would be required to close the budget gap and meet all debt payment obligations in 2022. While the city council approved these expenses, it was almost compelled to do this because a default on the Rose Bowl debt payments would damage the credit rating for other city borrowing so severely that it would also cost the city millions of dollars in the future.

Exceptional fundraising efforts emerged as the most promising solution to RBOC's financial challenges. An impressive, almost inspiring, sum of $40 million was raised from community boosters, sports enthusiasts, and historical preservation supporters. The total raised by the fundraising campaigns was almost as much as the $43 million in average annual revenues reported for each of the two years preceding the start of the pandemic in 2020.

Some creative responses to the challenges of the COVID-19 pandemic also helped to reduce budget pressures and retain experienced staff with quality event management skills. RBOC management introduced a drive-in theater onsite in July 2020 and continued offering more programs that built on the event's popularity. The new programs generated over $3 million in revenue and reduced the loss reported during the lockdown periods from $16 million to $13 million.

The 2022 Rose Bowl Game took place once again on New Year's Day as the Rose Bowl celebrated its 100th Anniversary. Despite the resurgence of COVID-19 infections caused by the Omicron variant, widespread vaccination protection against severe illness made it possible to accommodate a near capacity paid attendance of 87,842. The high attendance figure showed high pent-up demand by sports fans to attend live sports events, even with double-digit ticket price increases. RBOC could see that it would take years to recover the losses of the pandemic period, but the worst was over.

Whoop gained credibility from the use of its fitness tracking devices by sports event organizers as a means to monitor athlete health status. This strengthened the company's ability to launch in the German market in April 2022 when the FIBO sports business convention held its first live trade fair since 2019.

Photo by Max Donner at FIBO, Cologne, Germany April 8, 2022.

Key Sources and References

Aitken, P. February 7, 2022. "Super Bowl 2022 Ad Cost Hits New High: $7M for 30 Seconds in Biggest Ever Price Jump." *Fox Sports*.

Bruell, A. December 12, 2020. "TV Networks are Using ad Inventory to Make Good on Their Earlier Audience Commitments." *The Wall Street Journal*.

Carayol, T. December 14, 2020. "Tennis Adjusts to Covid New Normal With Smaller Events Facing Jeopardy." *The Guardian*.

KEY SOURCES AND REFERENCES 117

Carter, I. December 15, 2020, "European Tour: 18 Tournaments Return to 2021 Schedule." *BBC Sport.*

Deighton, K. November 3, 2020, "Emptied Sports Stadiums Tackle Losses with New Experiences." *The Wall Street Journal.*

Dixon, E. December 8, 2020. "NBA Hands Teams US$30m Each Ahead of 2020/21 Season." *SportsPro.*

Dixon, E. January 14, 2022, "Private property: Where do the top Sports Leagues Stand With Private Equity?" *SportsPro.*

Gillen, N. November 23, 2020. "FEI Predicting Loss of More Than CHF8 Million for 2020 as Direct Result of Pandemic." *Insidethegames.biz.*

Impey, S. September 29, 2020. "Report: MLB Suffers US$3bn Loss During Covid-Hit Season." *SportsPro.*

Ingle, S. December 30, 2020. "FA and RFU Lead Calls to get Grassroots Sport and Fans Back as Soon as Possible." *The Guardian.*

Makooi, B. December 3, 2020. "Covid-19: Forced to Close, French Ski Resorts Face 'Catastrophe' as Other Nations Keep Slopes Open." *France24.*

Owen, D. September 28, 2020. "International Bobsleigh and Skeleton Federation Budgets More Than $700,000 for COVID-19 in Current Financial Year." *Insidethegames.biz.* www.insidethegames.biz/articles/1098916/ibsf-coronavirus-expenses.

Pavitt, M. December 13, 2020. "French National Olympic and Sports Committee to Give Emergency Funding to 25 Federations." *Insidethegames.biz.*

Reinsch, M. August 8, 2020. "Corona-Hilfe Für Viele Ligen." *Frankfurter Allgemeine Zeitung.*

Ruiz, M. July 23, 2020. "DraftKings Study Found Sports Fans Divided About When to Return to Live Games, Have Social Distancing Concerns." *Fox Sports.*

Strougo, D. December 16, 2020. "Gym Owners Need Help. Congress Must Provide Relief or Fitness Industry Won't Make it: Community Gyms Coalition." *Fox Sports.*

Whitaker, W. December 6, 2020. "Some Colleges Axing "Secondary Sports" Like Gymnastics and Tennis as Pandemic Continues." *CBS 60 Minutes Sports.* www.cbsnews.com/news/college-sports-cuts-gymnastics-swimming-pandemic-60-minutes-2020-12-06/?fbclid=IwAR0SbPmyaBK07KzQt819QrvI1RP6KcDWa35yqSXrKnaRzPsweJ6JSW-n-7A.

CHAPTER 6

Virtual Reality

Perseverance

Top athletes like to be first. After COVID-19 was declared a global pandemic in March 2020, a new competition emerged to be the first major international sports competition among elite athletes. World Athletics' "Ultimate Garden Clash" won this race, and it also won attention for the future of virtual sports.

The "Ultimate Garden Clash" started on May 3, 2020. It featured pole vaulters Renaud Lavillenie, Sam Kendricks, and Mondo Du Plantis competing from their own backyards. The format was adapted to the pandemic with a simple "do-it-yourself" structure requiring no crew on site. The goal was to complete the highest number of 5 meter pole vaults in 30 minutes. No need to adjust the pole height; no need to change camera angles. Du Plantis and Lavillenie tied for first place with 36 vaults each. The live stream on World Athletics' YouTube channel attracted over 130,000 viewers. World Athletics reported that, in total, hundreds of thousands of spectators had seen segments of the special event on Instagram, Facebook, Twitter, and other social media.

The live stream of the second edition featuring female stars Katerina Stefanidi, Katie Nageotte, and Alysha Newman took place on May 16. It notched over 38,000 views on the World Athletics' YouTube channel. The format proved workable, although it did not get close to a world record for ratings.

The series continued on June 7 with decathlon stars Kevin Mayer, Niklas Kaul, and Maicel Uibo. This competition alternated pole vaults with shot put and shuttle run competitions. About 57,000 viewers watched the live stream.

The following week, on June 11, 2020, World Athletics restarted its top tier Diamond League series. Travel restrictions, quarantine requirements, and spectator limits all required flexibility and changes. Monaco accommodated 30 percent of the stadium's capacity, while Brussels and Stockholm followed local health requests and had no spectators at all. The production solution introduced by World Athletics for this novel challenge also highlighted a major drawback of the virtual sports format tested in the spring. World Athletics worked with audio technicians to design a stadium sound synthesis system that dynamically responded to results in competition as if a full crowd were present. For television audiences viewing professionally produced 90-minute television broadcasts, it was very close to the viewing experience they had grown to like. This was a feature that live-streamed webcasts from multiple remote locations could not match.

Experience with the virtual sports format became valuable as the pandemic wore on and became worse in many regions with Alpha and Delta variants, followed by Omicron outbreaks that caused top sports leagues like the NHL to cancel slates of games. Virtual sports might not be a first choice for fans, but they made it possible to keep competition calendars intact and for athletes to be able to train for peak performance. Savings in travel and facility costs earned virtual sports some points as well.

The International Weightlifting Federation (IWF) launched the first worldwide online weightlifting competition in autumn 2020. The live version of the IWF Youth World Championships had been scheduled for Lima, Peru, in November 2020. Peru's COVID-19 infection and death rates were among the highest in the world, and even athletes who could manage to travel there faced quarantines when they returned home. IWF rebranded the event as "IWF Youth World Cup." It adapted the format to a single series open to all national federations so that advance qualifying tournaments were incorporated into the single event. Over 400 athletes from 62 countries participated. The format change for this event was temporary, and the Youth World Championships returned to live competition in Heraklion, Greece, in May 2022.

Online competitions became part of the IWF toolkit after the concept was tested in 2020. It was chosen for the Commonwealth Games Qualifying Competition, the Oceania Junior + Youth Championships, and new "e-mail series" events in 2022. The cost savings made a difference to sports federations with limited budgets like IWF. The IWF's pre-pandemic financial forecasts in 2019 put annual revenues at about $2.5 million, less than total expenses.

Online competitions also helped Skate Canada maintain its operations when pandemic lockdowns forced the cancellation of live events in the winter of 2021. The entire country implemented a series of lockdowns that made local travel difficult and international travel subject to strict quarantines when re-entering Canada. A virtual competition appeared to be the only practical way to select skaters for the World Championships in Stockholm and World Team Trophy in Osaka later in 2021. The event debuted as the "Skate Canada Challenge."

The format Skate Canada selected was novel and unfamiliar for skaters and coaches, but it served its purpose. Skaters videotaped their competition routines at their home rinks with just coaches and a single video technician present. The videos were then sent online to judges who worked remotely, and scores were tallied virtually. The original plan had been to use the rankings to select competitors for the Canadian National Championships in Vancouver in February, but these were cancelled because of pandemic restrictions. Ultimately, the results of the "Skate Canada Challenge" were used to select the athletes for the international events in Stockholm and Osaka.

Virtual sports alternatives also demonstrated the potential for commercial sports operations to find ways to grow despite the challenges of a global pandemic. In 2021, the CrossFit organization launched the first ever CrossFit Occupational Games, using a 100 percent virtual competition format. The competition launched with six categories: college students plus military, law enforcement, firefighting, health care, and teaching professionals. This selection was a good match for large groups of potential participants whose schedules were not flexible enough to compete in person at regional events to compete in the CrossFit Games. Twenty thousand participants signed up for the program, which assigned workout challenges to be completed on video at home gyms or a local CrossFit box and uploaded for selection. The program was a success and was renewed for 2022.

For professional sports teams that expanded to include eSports teams as part of their fan engagement plans, audience interest remained modest. In spring 2022, Champions League football club Paris St. Germain had developed the largest following for its eSports team, but the virtual team's 188,000 followers on Instagram were just a small fraction of the primary club's 59 million followers. Likewise, the club eSports team of Bundesliga franchise Frankfurt Eintracht attracted just 12,000 Instagram followers, compared to 665,000 for the club as a whole.

Peloton Versus IRONMAN

Early in the pandemic, connected fitness and virtual sports attracted global attention as a key trend. Peloton, which had focused on connected fitness with virtual coaches training over a million subscribers at home, stood out as a model the sports industry could follow. The following two years were more like cycling over hilly terrain. Peloton lost $815 million in the second half of 2021, and its share price declined to prepandemic levels after rising as much as 500 percent during the pandemic. Its saga showed the sports industry that virtual sports had potential but that success was by no means guaranteed.

Peloton had certainly succeeded in demonstrating the viability of virtual platforms for fitness instruction at home. The total of 6.6 million paid subscribers it had signed up by the end of 2021 was 15 times the number of athletes participating in NCAA credentialed sports programs that year. But the company had management weaknesses well before the pandemic that resulted in continued financial losses. And the pandemic showed that its operations did not scale easily and were not well positioned for the sharp increase in consumer demand. Production and delivery failures accumulated, potential customers looked elsewhere, and a significant share of new customers did not hesitate to cancel their subscriptions when they had more choices after pandemic restrictions eased.

IRONMAN, which had established a long history of profitable operations before the pandemic, took a different approach to virtual sports and adapted. Its hybrid virtual and on-site model was established before the pandemic and was flexible enough to accommodate pandemic restrictions that resulted in the cancellation or postponement of most live sports competitions.

IRONMAN used virtual communication platforms to keep its community of athletes prepared and engaged. It started an in-house

IRONMAN Virtual Club and a virtual training service with a mobile phone app. In July 2020, the staff launched three different series of virtual races—a "Classic Division," a "Challenger Division," and a "Championship Series Division." Twenty-four races took place using the virtual format in July and August. The quick switch to a virtual format supported the retention of loyal participants, whose race entry fees, together with sponsorships, funded IRONMAN operations. This in turn enabled IRONMAN to retain some sports specialist staffers and coaching contractors to be positioned to return to growth when pandemic restrictions eased.

While the virtual format made it possible for IRONMAN to survive, the financial outlook was weak. Summer 2020 revenues declined by 87 percent from the same period in 2019, when live events dominated the activity calendar. The race organizer's holding company reported a modest net profit of $6.6 million, which was made possible by the lower costs of running virtual competitions. However, it became clear that a virtual-only business model could only support an organization a fraction of the enterprise's former scale.

IRONMAN live races returned to the sports calendar in full force in autumn 2021. By then, the virtual format was established well enough to continue as a profit center on its own. But live events quickly surpassed virtual ones in registrations and revenues. They featured important advantages that virtual formats had failed to deliver—excitement and enthusiasm.

Virtual sports faced another challenge to growth during the pandemic. Most of the growth in revenues in sports business was being generated by double-digit growth in sports betting. Some online sports betting operations, such as Betway, did hire category managers for online sports and added a few online events to the bets customers could place. But specialized expertise to forecast the odds of winning in virtual competitions was hard to find, and the low volumes did not leave surplus funds available for sponsorships.

When the 2020 season of the European eTour eSports series concluded in Dubai in January 2021, the numbers showed virtual sports as a niche that would face major challenges to grow into a full-fledged industry. Just 12,000 viewers watched the tournament live online.

And the total prize money of $50,000 was just 2 percent of the prize money offered at the European Masters Golf Tournament in Crans-Montana.

Olympic Breakthrough

Virtual formats proved valuable as substitutes for traditional sports activities when lockdowns and travel restrictions made adapting quickly a necessity. An opportunity for them to stand on their own and grow in the future emerged when the International Olympic Committee announced in April 2021 that it would launch a new initiative, the "Olympic Virtual Series."

The launch selected five sports. Cycling and rowing would take place as physical competitions using stationary equipment. Baseball, sailing, and motorsports would be produced as eSports competitions that simulated live sports events with split-second decision-making. The five sports selected had the advantage of a sports federation with relevant experience able to organize the events and monitor competition. And the series designated sports where an established publisher could standardize competition in multiple countries for an optimal "level playing field" experience.

The Olympic Virtual Series had an advantage that had eluded commercial virtual competitions. It had a clear motivation to grow the audience for sports and encourage participation. The series would become just one component of adding social media followers, scouting promising talent, and giving sports managers relevant experience in event promotion and operations. Participation was impressive for an international event that started just one month after the project was announced. 250,000 contestants competed.

The modest success of the first Olympic Virtual Series convinced IOC leaders to recruit full-time staff to manage the initiative. The new goal was to plan another series for 2022 and continue with promotions for the next Summer Olympics in Paris in 2024. The approach helped put virtual sports in perspective. Select sports where equipment and software can support fair competition and relatively simple broadcasting have potential and have a role to play in the sports ecosystem. Weightlifting has demonstrated its potential. But sports that require complex organization and facilities like whitewater canoeing or bobsleigh racing will be much more likely to remain traditional spectator sports.

A Case in Point: UCI Teams With Zwift

UCI, the international sports federation for cycling, had to cancel 650 events scheduled for 2020 because of pandemic restrictions and travel bans. Many top tier events that take place in a single country were adapted to pandemic restrictions and took place with careful COVID-19 prevention measures, including the Tour de France and Vuelta de Espana. But providing enough prize money and sponsor visibility opportunities for professional cyclists to keep racing was difficult and providing development opportunities for promising cyclists to qualify for top tier races faced even more obstacles.

Fortunately, UCI had already built a foundation for virtual competitions among cyclists using stationary exercise bikes connected over the Internet. UCI had entered a partnership with Zwift, a software developer of active eSports for at-home training and virtual competitions. The partnership began with Zwift simulating three real-life UCI Championship Courses for its subscribers to compete on. Then, in September 2019, UCI and Zwift announced that they would launch the UCI Cycling eSports World Championships in 2020.

While UCI struggled with the financial fallout of 650 race cancellations following the pandemic, Zwift flourished and was well positioned to support the multimillion dollar startup costs of organizing and publicizing the UCI Cycling eSports World Championships and help to develop eSports virtual competitions as a new category for UCI to add to live road and track races. Zwift's membership base grew 300 percent in the year following the COVID-19 pandemic. The increase in choices and value from the company's software apps also supported a 50 percent increase in monthly subscription fees over the basic service first offered in 2014. In September 2020, the company raised $450 million from private equity investors and surpassed $1 billion in total valuation.

The first UCI Cycling eSports World Championships began on December 9, 2020. The number of cyclists who signed up worldwide exceeded the most optimistic forecasts at over 193,000. The figure far surpassed the previous record for the world's largest virtual sports event, set two months earlier by the London Marathon. Zwift invested in promoting the event with podcasts featuring cycling stars and worked with UCI to arrange corporate sponsorship from Garmin-Tacx, Shimano,

Toyota, and Science in Sport, a sports nutrition specialist. At the same time, Zwift organized and promoted another mass participation competition, the "Nations Challenge." This attracted riders from countries around the world and awarded international rankings based on the fastest average times achieved by cyclists from each country.

This large-scale demonstration of how a virtual cycling competition could complement traditional cycling events set the stage for expansion of UCI's partnership with Zwift. The Movistar Team of the UCI World Cycling tour started recruiting cyclists for its eSports development team using the Zwift platform for recruiting and event management. UCI and Zwift extended the UCI Cycling eSports World Championships, with qualifying races in 2021 and the finals in February 2022. Then Zwift was designated the official gaming publisher of the cycling competitions in the first ever Olympic Virtual Series, scheduled for May and June of 2021.

The IOC selected five sports for the launch of the virtual series, including cycling, and selected UCI chief David Lappartient to lead the entire virtual sports effort. A track record of successful implementation with experienced game publishers was a key criterion for selection, and UCI's history of working with Zwift was advantageous. The Olympic Virtual Series achieved another goal. It concluded on Olympic Day, June 23, and made it possible for supporters to organize online events without concerns about local restrictions on large gatherings.

As the Olympic Virtual Series concluded, Zwift announced a four-year agreement with a prestigious UCI World Tour series, the Tour de France. Zwift became the presenting partner of a new eight-day women's competition for the Tour de France.

In a classic win-win outcome, the partnership between UCI and Zwift achieved benefits for both organizations.

UCI gained:

- A new competition category that helped to expand its global reach
- Flexibility to organize races independent of COVID-19 gathering size restrictions or travel bans
- A program that added participation opportunities to cyclists from smaller countries that do not have the resources to support a local competition series

- An alternative for talent development to give professional cycling teams an opportunity to observe and recruit promising junior cyclists
- A more active means to engage retired professional cyclists

Zwift gained:

- Prestige for its platform as a competitive advantage versus other subscription services, notably Peloton
- Product trials of its subscription services by more competitive cyclists to help grow its subscriber base
- Visibility on The Olympic Channel and with Olympic broadcast partners worldwide
- Additional rider contact lists and rider performance data to upsell other services and develop new product offerings
- Course data from well-known UCI World Tour races to design eSports races with strong appeal and name recognition in the global cycling community

The global COVID-19 pandemic created new opportunities for technology enterprises to develop virtual alternatives for sports and fitness, connected in the Metaverse.

Photo by Max Donner at FIBO, Cologne, Germany April 8, 2022.

Key Sources and References

Gillen, N. November 21, 2020. "Are Virtual Sport Events Here to Stay?" *insidethegames.biz*. www.insidethegames.biz/articles/1101051/are-virtual-sport-events-here-to-stay.

Houston, M. December 12, 2021. "Olympic Virtual Series to Return for 2022 Following Successful Inaugural Year." *insidethegames.biz*. www.insidethegames.biz/articles/1116728/olympic-virtual-series-ioc.

Ingle, S. May 3, 2020. "Duplantis and Lavillenie Scale the Heights in Ultimate Garden Clash." *The Guardian*. www.theguardian.com/sport/2020/may/03/duplantis-and-lavillenie-scale-the-heights-in-ultimate-garden-clash.

Ingle, S. April 22, 2021. "IOC launches Olympic Virtual Series." *The Guardian*. www.theguardian.com/sport/2021/apr/22/virtual-olympic-series-launched-ioc-baseball-cycling-rowing.

Murphy, J. October 2, 2021. "Pandemic's Peloton Obsession Turns to Peloton Fatigue." *The Wall Street Journal*.

CHAPTER 7

Olympic Records

Going for the Gold

At the age of 25, Canadian snowboarder Max Parrot earned a silver medal in the snowboard slopestyle competition at the 2018 Winter Olympics in Pyeongchang. Four years later, he won his first Olympic gold medal in the same event. The achievement was also Canada's first gold medal at the 2022 Winter Olympic Games. That was impressive enough, but Max Parrot's extraordinary efforts to get on the podium again showed the Olympic spirit at its best. Parrot had battled lymphatic cancer the year after his Pyeongchang 2018 success and had to miss the entire 2018–2019 season.

Max Parrot's triumph over lymphatic cancer symbolized what could still be possible in the COVID-19 pandemic era. This disease typically weakens the immune system so aggressively that it would make any patient a high-risk individual for severe COVID-19 or a fatal outcome. Some diagnosed with this terrible malady could only survive the COVID-19 pandemic by isolating and sheltering in place. Parrot was able to persist with 12 series of chemotherapy treatments, a painstaking physical rehabilitation regimen, a return to training, and then, ten months later, a return to elite competition. He won a gold medal at the 2020 Winter X-Games and found inspiration to continue his dramatic comeback through the many challenges of the COVID-19 pandemic.

Niklas Edin, who led Sweden's gold medal winning curling team at Beijing 2022, had to overcome major injuries for decades. He suffered a herniated disk when he was 14 and had a total of ten operations before he competed at the 2022 Winter Olympics. His championship success sent a hopeful message to millions of others battling chronic health conditions that they, too, could find solutions to be productive and achieve their goals.

The power of this kind of inspiration is just one element of many needed to enable the world to function as long as COVID-19 circulates. But few institutions have shown the longevity and resilience of the Olympics. That meant that finding ways to continue producing the Olympics despite the massive challenges posed by the COVID-19 pandemic had unique value.

Max Parrot and Niklas Edin had esteemed company in overcoming serious illness to persevere at the Olympics. Three-time snowboarding Olympic gold medalist Shaun White did not win a medal at Beijing 2022. He did achieve a respectable fourth-place finish in the half-pipe which was all the more impressive because White had just recently recovered from a symptomatic case of COVID-19. White had completed full vaccination to be able to compete at Beijing 2022, but he tested positive just before Christmas 2021 as case numbers in the United States rose in a new wave. His illness developed similarly to other postvaccination "breakthrough" cases with fever and fatigue. But it could have been much worse; White had previously suffered from asthma and a heart condition, medical conditions that had been observed to increase the risk of severe COVID-19 cases. White pulled through and tested negative twice before the U.S. Olympic trials on January 7, 2022, and he earned his place at the Winter Olympics.

Bobsledder Elana Meyers Taylor overcame the challenge of testing positive for COVID-19 after her arrival in Beijing for the 2022 Winter Olympics. She had also completed full vaccination to be able to enter the "closed loop" biosecure enclave created to contain the risk of spreading COVID-19 infections. Meyers had to quarantine during the Beijing 2022 Opening Ceremony and miss the honor of carrying the U.S. flag during the ceremony. But she recovered quickly enough to test negative and continue competing. Her efforts brought the first Olympic gold medal in women's monobob and an historic fifth Olympic medal on February 19.

Skier William Flaherty did not win any Olympic medals, but he overcame a serious health challenge that made his achievement of finishing two Olympic races stand out. The 17-year-old athlete from Puerto Rico had battled hemophagocytic lymph histiocytosis (HLH), a rare condition that carried serious risk for severe COVID-19 and was often fatal in itself. The condition causes the immune system to attack the body's organs. Flaherty finished in 40th place in the men's giant slalom and 42nd in his final Alpine skiing race. In the COVID-19 pandemic era, just finishing a sports competition or sports event took on new value as billions of people looked for ways to overcome the exceptional challenges of this period.

The extraordinary efforts made to adapt to the COVID-19 pandemic so that the Olympics could take place in Tokyo and Beijing and keep the institution intact for the Paris 2024 Summer Olympics were burdensome, expensive, and had no guarantee of success. But they added two more major events to the list of finishers. They also showed how many others could manage.

An Epic Challenge

The ancient Olympics paid tribute to the Greek god Hercules, and the strength and perseverance he demonstrated in many trials. The COVID-19 pandemic magnified the drama of epic challenges.

It had taken a decade to plan and build for the Tokyo 2020 Summer Olympics. The budget exceeded $10 billion. The training and selection of the top athletes to compete was a worldwide effort that involved over 100,000 athletes, coaches, officials, and support staff to make it possible. Reconfiguring these efforts to accommodate a myriad of restrictions developed to keep the pandemic under control appeared so complicated that many observers viewed cancellation as the only practical solution. The leadership of the International Olympic Committee and the local organizing committee in Tokyo recognized that major changes would be necessary and determined to find workable solutions.

While the Olympic Games planned for 1916, 1940, and 1944 had been cancelled outright because of wars and individual Olympic events had been postponed briefly, no entire Olympic Games had ever been postponed before. In the spring of 2020, the IOC Executive Committee decided that a postponement of the Summer Olympics for one year and holding the 2022 Winter Olympics on the dates planned was the most workable solution to preserve the strengths of the organization and the expertise needed to train athletes for Olympic sports. No one said that it would be easy.

To move forward with plans for Tokyo 2020, the organizing committee established a postponement task force. Its assignment was to systematically identify all the thousands of tasks that would need to be completed to present the Games and 339 sporting competitions in 2021. Details accumulated quickly. Physical facilities to present the competitions needed to be secured, the conversion of the Athlete's Village to private residences needed to be postponed, and telecommunications facilities for broadcasting events needed to be reserved. And detailed contingency plans for transporting and housing athletes safely during a global health crisis needed to be in place.

Only half of the competitions for selecting the athletes to compete in the Olympics had been completed, so a massive rescheduling of qualifying events and modification of qualifying selection procedures became a huge project of its own. This was also a moving target. The International Triathlon Union had scheduled its Olympic qualifying event for May 2020 in Chengdu, China. In February, it arranged to move the event to Valencia, Spain, on May 1 and 2. Spain was still in a strict lockdown in May 2020, so the competition was postponed until November 7, 2020, in Valencia.

Some schedule changes will alter the international sports calendar through 2024. FINA, the international aquatic sports federation, had scheduled its 19th World Championships in July 2021 in Fukuoka, Japan. The original event was postponed to May 2022 to accommodate the dates for the rescheduled Tokyo 2020 Olympics. In winter 2022, as Japan continued international travel restrictions, FINA postponed the event once again to July 2023 in Fukuoka, Japan. The 20th FINA World Championships had been scheduled for 2023 in Doha, but the event was rescheduled to 2024 to accommodate the series of changes.

The ability of golf, athletics, football, and a few other sports to restart the competition calendar by June 2020 showed that there were options for hosting sports events during a pandemic, but the Olympics and Paralympics plans for Tokyo were a completely different order of magnitude, involving over 18,000 athletes. To move forward, organizers developed and promoted a "Playbook." This was basically a rigid set of procedures based on the experience of sports events that had already adapted to the pandemic and demonstrated the ability to avoid COVID-19 outbreaks.

The final Playbook issued in June 2021 tried to reassure the community with past results from 430 major sports events since September 2020, with over 54,000 athletes in total participating. This included test events held in Japan in May—the International Volleyball Games Tokyo Challenge 2021, the FINA Diving World Cup 2021, the Hokkaido + Sapporo Marathon Festival 2021, and "READY STEADY TOKYO" Athletics. There were no positive COVID-19 tests after arrival testing among the 700 athletes and 6,000 support staff and media participating. This result built confidence that the revised plan for Tokyo 2020 would work, although the IOC press office also worked to build expectations that some positive cases would be reported and that measures would focus on preventing the further spread of any isolated infections.

The May 2021 test events had not allowed spectators, and ultimately, spectators were excluded from almost all Tokyo 2020 competitions. Cycling events held in a sparsely populated resort area on the Izu Peninsula did allow local fans to buy tickets and attend with social distancing. This had the additional advantage that there was at least some material for video and photo archives that showed a traditional celebratory atmosphere at the Games.

The Playbook strategy planned a modified bubble with multiple locations, similar to the approach that had proven feasible at the Men's International Handball World Championships in January. COVID-19 testing upon arrival and frequently thereafter would be used to isolate infections and prevent outbreaks from occurring. Transportation between sites would be exclusively for participants who were prohibited from using public transit. Journalists and support staff not housed in the Athlete's Village had to limit their contacts to select preapproved locations and keep trips outside the bubble under 15 minutes. By this time, there was a body of scientific evidence backing the strategy of keeping contacts under 15 minutes to prevent new infections. When put to the test at Tokyo 2020, it actually worked. Playbook rules were not recommendations; they were mandatory rules with substantial penalties for noncompliance.

Vaccination against COVID-19 was not mandatory, but it was strongly encouraged. The IOC secured a donation of 40,000 additional doses for athletes, support staff, and media from Pfizer/BioNTech, which was produced with shift adjustments so that it did not reduce the supplies of vaccines available to the general public.

While most of the sports community was willing to make sacrifices to move forward with the postponed Olympics, many residents of the host region and host country had differing perspectives. By international comparisons, Japan had avoided a severe health crisis. Japan's mortality rate of 40 COVID-19 deaths per million was a small fraction of the rate of 1,281 per million in the United States during the first year of the pandemic and not higher than a bad flu season. For most of 2020, Japan had managed to conduct professional sports with spectator attendance limits. Traditional "test, trace, and quarantine" approaches that had controlled the SARS outbreak in Toronto in 2003 helped to keep the health risks under control.

Then, in 2021, the more contagious Alpha variant emerged, followed by the even more contagious Delta variant. Japan's timeframe and capacity for vaccinating most of the population against COVID-19 were uncertain, but widespread vaccination protection before the planned start of the Summer Olympics was unlikely. Public concern about hosting the Olympics mounted, and then even sponsors came forward to advocate cancellation of the games. In late May, the Asahi Shinbun, an official sponsor of Tokyo 2020, called for the Games to be cancelled, calling plans to hold them "a gamble."

The COVID-19 pandemic did not just raise concerns about infections spreading from international visitors to the local population. Local hospitals risked exceeding capacity limits. Tokyo 2020 organizers adjusted medical team staffing to reduce personnel by about 30 percent and make more medical professionals available for local health care duties.

Implementing extraordinary COVID-19 prevention policies at Tokyo 2020 was expensive. *The Wall Street Journal* estimated that the direct material and personnel costs for COVID-19 screening plus quarantine facilities reached $68 million. Foregone revenues from the inability to sell tickets to spectators were estimated at $800 million.

While only 70 percent to 80 percent of foreign participants were vaccinated, Tokyo 2020 recorded an infection rate of just 0.02 percent from 624,000 samples. Most positive cases were among local workers who were infected while commuting or through local contacts; only 29 athletes returned positive tests and needed to isolate themselves and change their competition plans. There were no outbreaks linked to Tokyo 2020 participants and zero deaths.

While the Tokyo 2020 story of COVID-19 prevention was a success story for public health managers, it was not a story that engaged television audiences. Many potential viewers were saturated with COVID-19 news, uncertain what Olympic events they would be able to view, and preoccupied with returning to their offices and family events once restrictions in their own countries were phased out. The results were uneven and made the challenge of activating sponsorships and planning broadcast programming and interviews even more complicated.

The streaming results provided some good news—and more world records. BBC Sport registered 104 million users for its webcasts compared to 68.3 million at Rio 2016; both figures exceeded the UK's total population of 67 million as fans connected computers, tablets, and smartphones and tried out the experience of viewing multiple broadcasts simultaneously. This "second screen" phenomenon added another dimension of complexity for sponsors trying to improve their visibility and for sports federations trying to win new supporters and athletic talent for their sports.

Streaming figures from the U.S. market also set new records. American viewers streamed a record total of 5.5 billion minutes of NBC's coverage from the broadcaster's social media webcasts and online platforms such as NBCOlympics.com, the Golf Channel, the NBC Sports app, and the broadcast conglomerate's in-house streaming service "Peacock." This supported the marketing objective of using the Olympics to get new users to try out new services.

From the perspective of broadcasters using the Olympics to win new customers for paid subscriber services, the results were spectacular. These results also set new records. Eurosport reported that new subscriptions grew by 300 percent over the 2018 Winter Olympics.

The decline in the scale of the global broadcast audience was similar to that of major league sports that had also postponed their schedules. Just over three billion viewers watched some live Olympics coverage broadcast by an official broadcast partner. That was notably less than 3.6 million viewers for the London 2012 Olympics and 3.2 million for the Rio 2016 Olympics.

The global broadcast results were uneven. Host country Japan as well as Australia, in a nearby time zone, reported good growth. In Australia, daily viewership ranged from 7 to 20 percent higher than Rio 2016. Japan's audience of 70 million for the opening ceremony was the highest for any program in the past ten years. Sweden and Norway also reported new records for individual broadcasts of highly anticipated finals.

In the United States, the Summer Olympic Games averaged 15.5 million prime-time TV viewers during 17 days of network broadcasts. That marked a 42 percent decline from the Rio de Janeiro Olympics in 2016. But the figure was also larger than television audiences for all professional sports in North America, except for the NFL. In the UK, official broadcaster BBC's television audience for the 2020 Summer Olympics dropped to the lowest figure since 2004, reaching just 36.4 million viewers.

France's public broadcaster reported a 17 percent decline in viewership over 2016, despite enthusiastic advance publicity and events for hosting the next Summer Olympics in Paris in 2024. Part of the local broadcaster's audience decline was compensated by additional coverage on the Eurosport Channel, accessible with paid subscriptions in 50 European countries, including France. But a visible part of the decline reflected saturation of interest in watching television by millions of people who had been confined to their homes during four strict lockdowns that added up to 30 weeks in red zones.

Tokyo 2020 set another record as the most expensive Summer Olympics to date. The original estimate put forth by the Tokyo 2020 local organizing committee was $7.4 billion. Prior to COVID-19 being declared a global pandemic in 2020, the cost estimate had already increased to $12.8 billion. Final figures that included additional staffing, facilities, and health costs resulting from the one year postponement pushed the final accounting over $13.6 billion. There had been concerns that total expenses would be even higher, but expenses to provide services for spectators were cut from the plan along with the Nippon Festival promotion of cultural events, resulting in over $1.5 billion in cost reductions.

More traditional sports records polished the image of the Tokyo 2020 Olympics and presented a vision of a steady recovery from the worst of the COVID-19 pandemic. A total of 23 new world records were set by athletes competing at the Summer Olympic Games. Lasha Talakhadze, a weightlifter, set three different world records at Tokyo 2020. Caeleb Dressel of Team USA set two new world records in swimming. At the men's 400 meter hurdles final, the previous world record was shattered twice in quick succession. Then, at the women's 400 meter hurdles final, Sydney McLaughlin beat her own world record by 46 hundredths of a second. Yulimar Rojas of Venezuela set a new world record in the women's triple-jump competition and became the first female athlete from Venezuela to win an Olympic gold medal.

The results from the Tokyo 2020 Paralympic Games were even more impressive. The event itself earned an entry in the Guinness Book of World Records for the largest athlete participation in a multisport adaptive sport event—with 4403 athletes. Sixty-nine new world records were set in swimming competitions alone. The total number of new world records set in ten days of competition reached 182.

Paralympic world record setting champions showed the world that determination, discipline, and effort could overcome health challenges to achieve ambitious goals:

- Emily Petricola of Australia battled multiple sclerosis, but she managed to win a gold medal and set a new world record in track cycling's Paralympic 3,000 meter contest.
- Anastasia Pagonis of Team USA is blind and diagnosed with an autoimmune disorder, but she set a new world record in the 400 meter freestyle swimming competition at the age of 17.
- American sprinter Nick Mayhugh was born with cerebral palsy. This health challenge did not stand in his way, setting a Paralympic world record of 10.95 seconds in the 100 meter dash and setting a new world record in the 200 meter competition the following week.
- American swimmer Robert Griswold was also diagnosed with cerebral palsy; he won a Paralympic gold medal and set a new world record in the 100 meter backstroke competition.

The frequency of success at Tokyo 2020, and the achievement of completing all medal events on schedule, built confidence that the sports world could rise to the continuing challenges posed by the COVID-19 pandemic. The next challenge was daunting, even by Olympic standards. That was to be 100 percent prepared for the Beijing 2022 Winter Olympics to start just five months after the conclusion of the Tokyo 2020 Paralympic Games.

A New Great Wall

Unlike Tokyo 2020, Beijing 2022 did not hold any test events with international athletes and staffing the two years before the games. Facilities were tested with local athletes and media in what were described as "adaptive events." The approach worked well enough to support technical excellence in presenting the Games but did not provide a solution for COVID-19 control at the Games themselves.

Ultimately, the strategy to prevent COVID-19 outbreaks selected by Beijing 2022 organizers and local health authorities was presented as a "closed loop." International participants had to arrive in Beijing on direct flights after showing proof of vaccination plus a negative PCR test (considered the gold standard in COVID-19 testing). Arrivals were required to take dedicated transport to accommodations, training facilities, and, of course, COVID-19 testing facilities for daily tests. Travel outside the "closed loop" was prohibited. The vaccination requirement exempted dozens of teenage athletes who lived in countries where no vaccine had yet obtained regulatory approval for their age group.

The volume of COVID-19 testing set a record of its own—1.8 million tests administered in a four-week period for a single event. Over 4,000 athletes and coaches, plus 62,000 support staff, from housekeepers to lighting technicians, were on the testing roster. The total number of positive tests reported before the Games concluded was 437, with most positive cases found on arrival in Beijing and isolated quickly. The positive rate was three times higher than that reported in Tokyo the previous summer, reflecting the higher infectiousness of the Omicron variant and the peak of global infections in the winter of 2022.

The "closed loop" policy also excluded international spectators. No cheering fans, no cowbell clangs, no beaming parents in the stands. Athletes benefit from motivation to achieve peak performance, and while some found new ways to connect with fans and gain their support on social media, that was not a universal solution. The alternative chosen, to invite prescreened local residents to watch live events in blocks of seating spaced to minimize contacts, was not designed for enthusiasm, and it showed.

China's "closed loop" procedures worked effectively to prevent outbreaks and prevent any infections experienced by foreign visitors from spreading to the local population. They worked so well that China's decision makers announced plans to follow them again for the international sports competitions China was planning in the future. But with the high incidence of the highly contagious Omicron variant in the winter of 2022, COVID-19 wreaked havoc on competition plans, athlete training, and Olympics management. Infections were reported and screened out at a rapid pace:

- Jake Sanderson of the U.S. Men's Hockey Team tested positive when he arrived in Los Angeles to join the team for training; after isolating and then testing negative, he traveled separately to join the team in Beijing without the benefit of advance practice with his teammates.
- Vincent Zhou, a Team USA figure skater, tested negative upon arrival in Beijing and before the team event he competed in; he then tested positive for COVID-19, was confined to a quarantine hotel, and missed the two individual events for which he had qualified.
- The Canada versus Russian Athletes women's hockey matchup barely had enough players to take place after one Canadian and six Russian players tested positive for COVID-19.
- Russia's bobsledders Aleksei Pushkarev and Vasiliy Kondratenko, skeleton racer Nikita Tregubov, ice skaters Egor Bazin and Mikhail Kolyada, as well as ice hockey center Artem Anisimov all tested positive before departure and had to isolate themselves and attempt to continue training on their own.
- Paris 2024 President Tony Estanguet tested positive for COVID-19 at the end of January 2022 and isolated with

mild symptoms, causing him to cancel a planned trip to the start of the 2022 Winter Olympics and the 139th session of the International Olympic Committee, where more decisions for Paris 2024 were finalized.

IOC member Princess Anne of Great Britain also did not attend the 139th session of the International Olympic Committee because of conflicts with travel restrictions. Just three-quarters of the voting members of the IOC were able to travel to and from Beijing to participate in the meetings and election of new members.

The sagas of Olympic athletes who had contracted COVID-19 before the games and recovered in time to compete were perplexing and inevitably affected advance training. With much of the world audience facing similar challenges their recoveries offered a bit of inspiration, but the results were mixed. Mikaela Shiffrin, a two-time Olympic Gold medalist and 73-time World Cup winner at the start of Beijing 2022, had contracted COVID-19 at the end of December 2021. Shiffrin returned to competition January 4 and placed second in her first race of the year, but her performance at Beijing 2022 was disappointing. She did not finish three of the five races she started and placed ninth in one race and 18th in the other.

At the last Team USA Olympic qualifying event for figure skaters held in Nashville in early January, three top athletes returned positive tests and needed to be isolated: Brandon Frazier, Amber Glenn, and Alysa Liu. All three cases were unnerving, because the athletes had been vaccinated and tested negative for COVID-19 before their departure for Nashville. Afterwards, Brandon Frazier joined the list of inspirational COVID-19 recovery success stories when he won a silver medal in pairs figure skating at Beijing 2022. Alysa Liu recovered in time to join the U.S. team at Beijing 2022, where she placed seventh and eighth in two events. Two months later, at the age of 16, she announced that she was retiring from figure skating. Amber Glenn performed well enough earlier in the season to earn a place as an alternate on the U.S. figure skating team, but she reported suffering for weeks from COVID-19 complications.

Exceptional weather helped to brighten the outlook. Winter is normally a dry season in the Beijing area, and artificial snow was produced in world record quantities to ensure the outdoor sports could take place on the custom designed courses. But picturesque natural snowfall covered the area in time for most outdoor events and sparkled for audiences around the world.

Athletes also sparkled and set new world records. Nils van der Poel of Sweden surpassed his own world record in the men's 10,000 meter speed skating finals, clocking 12 minutes and 30.74 seconds. Suzanne Schulting broke the previous world record in women's 1,000 meter speed skating in 1 minute and 1:26.514 seconds. Figure skaters made history with record high scores: Nathan Chen (113.97 in the men's individual event short program), followed by the figure skating pair of Sui Wenjing and Han Cong (84.41 in the pairs short program), and then world champions Gabriella Papadakis and Guillaume Cizeron of France, who scored 90.83 points in the rhythm dance program of the ice dance competition.

Resilience: The Key Success Factor in Sports

As the sports world moved forward after the exceptional Olympics held in Tokyo and Beijing, what did not happen became as important as what did happen. Corporate sponsors did not shorten or cancel their support. Broadcast partners did not terminate their contracts or seek refunds. Broadcasters did not lose money as savings from remote production and smaller staffs buffered some declines in viewership. Athletes did not stop training. Olympic hopefuls did not stop dreaming.

What the sports world and most of the rest of the world did see is a quality that has become even more important during the COVID-19 pandemic—resilience. Athletes faced closure of their training facilities, frequent postponements and cancellations, personal financial difficulties, and often total confinement to their homes and physical separation from their teammates. As one after another set new world records, as one after another contracted COVID-19 and then recovered, millions of ordinary citizens trying to get on with their daily lives could see resilient role models who would not let COVID-19 defeat them.

A Case in Point: Paris 2024 Aims to Make the Olympic Flame Shine

Paris 2024 started with ambitious goals for greatly reducing the expenses of hosting the Olympics and Paralympics, with a focus on using existing facilities. The COVID-19 pandemic made this goal all the more important as the exceptional measures to cope with the pandemic at Tokyo 2020 and Beijing 2022 pressured budgets at the same time that spectator revenues disappeared. The Paris 2024 organization responded with an optimistic approach that combined reducing expenses for some facilities while aggressively pursuing objectives for mass participation and promotion of sports to maximize public engagement and support for its vision.

Even with a systematic approach to keep expenses under control, financial projections for Paris 2024 were significant and kept rising. At the end of 2021, the budget for new facilities and improvements to existing facilities was 3.4 billion euros, with 1.1 billion euros of public funds set aside to secure their use for the period after the Games. The operating budget for the organizing committee was 3.9 billion euros. The promised contribution from the IOC was 1.1 billion euros, leaving 2.8 billion euros to be financed by other sources. Optimistic projections forecast that 1 to 1.5 billion euros could be generated from ticket sales and other spectator and merchandising revenues. The total forecast expenditures of 7.3 billion euros marked a 10 percent increase over the original forecast submitted to the IOC when bidding to host the games.

The COVID-19 pandemic made financing ambitious plans for Paris 2024 even more challenging. At the end of 2021, the city of Paris estimated that the city's total debt would approach 9 billion euros after the Games and would take 35 years to repay if the Games avoided any cost overruns that Paris would have to cover because of its guarantees. At the same time, pledges for corporate sponsorships had reached 600 million euros, leaving an additional 500 million euros to be raised to meet the original target for this source of funding.

The sharp rise in inflation that followed the large extra expenses the French government incurred to manage critical measures during the COVID-19 pandemic added a new challenge. By the end of 2021, the construction program manager reported that expenditures were already higher than original forecasts; a 300 million euro contingency reserve in the budget did not address inflation at this level.

Select choices for reducing expenditures appeared modest by comparison. Eliminating two venues planned as temporary facilities could save 60 million euros. Using a large existing stadium in the city of Lille, an hour and 15 minutes from Paris by train, was selected for similar savings for handball matches. Another 60 million euro expense reduction was anticipated from introducing innovative "venue Twin" software to model event plans for the different locations that will be used for the Paris 2024 Olympics. The possibility of achieving more cost savings by using the national shooting sports center several hours away from Paris offered more economies, but this raised logistical and operational concerns.

Exploring alternate approaches to raising more revenues confronted the financial realities of a world recovering from the COVID-19 pandemic. The Olympic torch relay sought to raise 15 million euros with a contribution from each local region of France as part of a plan to stage the event throughout the country. Several regions simply could not manage the additional expense after two years of extraordinary COVID-19 expenses.

The challenging financial outlook became one more reason to find ways to strengthen the Paris 2024 brand, seek higher visibility in both traditional media and digital media channels, and reach out to new audiences that could deliver enhanced value for sponsors and supporters. Paris 2024 launched a membership organization, the Paris 2024 Club, with communications and events leading up to the Games. For the first time ever, the closing ceremony of the Summer Olympic Games took place in two cities, with Paris presenting a spectacular show for the handover from Tokyo 2020. Supporters filled the fan zone around the Eiffel Tower, star athletes generated enthusiasm, and a brilliant aerial display added excitement for the "City of Lights."

As plans moved forward, the organizing committee promoted a big start and finish for the 2024 Summer Olympic Games. The Opening Ceremony will take place with a fleet procession down the Seine River in the heart of Paris so that 600,000 spectators can see the event in person. The Games will conclude with a mass participation marathon on the same day and course as the final marathon race, just before the closing ceremony. The large events also opened new sponsorship opportunities to capitalize on the high visibility and make a modest contribution to keeping the multibillion dollar budget manageable.

The Paris 2024 plan achieved a notable advantage. Public support in the host country reached near record levels of approval by the end of the Tokyo 2020 Paralympics, reported at 90 percent in the most favorable survey. This provided a foundation for the confidence factor to guide the local organizing staff and volunteers past the many challenges that continued to arise on a regular basis. This gave them a unique opportunity to demonstrate resilience for the sports world and for their city and build hope that the "City of Lights" could also be the light at the end of the tunnel.

Paris 2024 CEO Tony Estanguet and the Paris 2024 team faced an Olympic-sized challenge to continue implementing plans for the 2024 Summer Olympics while the global pandemic restricted travel and meetings over a two-year period. Continued success is inspiring other sports organizations to raise the bar and set new records.

Photo by Max Donner at Global Sports Week, Paris, France, May 10, 2022.

Key Sources and References

Anthony, E. August 8, 2021. "Mixed bag: Erratic Pandemic Olympics Come to a Nuanced end." *The Japan Times*.

Associated Press. February 12, 2022. "Olympic Skier Overcomes Illness to Compete for Puerto Rico." *Fox News*.

Barker, P. February 8, 2022. "Beijing 2022 Proving to be Hit in Sweden, but IOC Paymasters NBC Continuing to Struggle." *Insidethegames.biz*.

Cacciola, S. February 14, 2022. "A Curler Chases Gold, While He Still Can." *The New York Times*.

Dichter, M. February 7, 2022. "Snowboarder Max Parrot Soars to Canada's 1st Gold Medal at Beijing Olympics." *CBC Sports*.

Flood, B. July 28, 2021. "NBC's Tokyo Olympics Coverage Spurs 'Advertiser Anxiety' as Viewership Continues to Decline." *Fox News*.

Flood, B. August 10, 2021. "NBC Tokyo Olympics Ratings 'Faceplanted,' Finishes With Smallest Summer Games Audience in Network History." *Fox News*.

Liang, R. February 19, 2022. "One of the Hardest Feats at the Winter Olympics Is Calculating the Bill." *The Wall Street Journal*.

Prat, J. January 7, 2022. "Shaun White Shares That he Tested Positive for Covid." *IOC Newroom*. https://olympics.com/en/news/shaun-white-positive-covid-test-result.

Reuters News Agency. February 17, 2022. "Beijing Olympics Reports No New COVID-19 Cases for the First Time." *The Japan Times*.

Ruiz, M. August 7, 2021." NBC Sees 'Worst Case Scenario' as Olympics Ratings Plunge." *Fox News*.

Rutz, D. February 21, 2022. "NBC's Beijing Olympic Ratings Called a 'Disaster' for Network." *Fox News*.

Yu, C. August 8, 2021. "A Look at All of the World Records That Were Broken at the Tokyo Olympics." *The New York Times*.

Glossary

ATP	(Association of Tennis Professionals) Organizer of the most prestigious international tournaments for men's professional tennis
COVID-19	Severe illness caused by a strain of coronavirus which emerged in 2019 which can be asymptomatic, but can also result in severe acute respiratory syndrome and aggravate other severe maladies
FIFA	(Federation International de Football) International sports federation organizing international football competitions including the Men's and Women's Football World Cups and continental competitions of national teams
FIVB	(Federation International de Volleyball) International sports federation organizing international volleyball competitions
Formula One	Sports event manager for international automobile racing contests
IOC	(International Olympic Committee) Sports organization which presents the Summer Olympic Games, Winter Olympic Games and Youth Olympic Games, and also selects the international sports federations and host cities which participate
IPC	(International Paralympic Committee) Sports organization which presents global competitions for athletes in sports adapted to significant physical challenges which require specialized equipment and facilities
IPL	(Indian Premiere League) Sports league based in India which schedules competitions between professional cricket teams and sets rules and standards for competitions

MLB	(Major League Baseball) Sports league based in North America which schedules competitions between professional baseball teams and sets rules and standards for competitions
MLS	(Major League Soccer) Sports league based in North America which schedules competitions between professional soccer teams and sets rules and standards for competitions
NCAA	(National Collegiate Athletic Association) Governing body of amateur sports at colleges and universities in North America
NFL	(National Football League) Sports league based in North America which schedules competitions between professional teams in the sport of American football and sets rules and standards for competitions
NHL	(National Hockey League) Sports league based in North America which schedules competitions between professional ice hockey teams and sets rules and standards for competitions
Private equity	Form of financing business activities by using pools of funds raised from private investors to acquire ownership shares which have rights to share in future profits
WTA	(Women's Tennis Association) Organizer of the most prestigious international tournaments for women's professional tennis
WHO	(World Health Organization) United Nations Agency which reports on global health trends and connects medical experts to share information regarding health crises that extend beyond national borders

About the Author

Max Donner is a private equity investment analyst and a widely published author of magazine features and interviews. He began his publishing career as a stock market columnist and followed reader interest to add two decades of in-depth sports business coverage as well as the book *The Olympic Sports Economy*. He studied economics at Amherst College and Cornell University and finance at Harvard Business School, where he was awarded an MBA degree with honors.

Index

"Adria Tour," 73
All Blacks, 95–96
America's Cup, 39, 40
ATP World Tour, 65, 67–69
Australian Open, 51, 79

Belmont Stakes, 57
Biosecure bubble, 26–29, 53
Border closures, 11

CAA World Congress of Sports, 44
CVC Capital Partners, 98
Cardiovascular Research Institute of the University of Virginia, 72
ClassPass, 87
"Closed loop" policy, 138–139
Corona Warn App, 59
CrossFit Occupational Games, 121
Cyber workouts, 17, 90

Data-driven artificial intelligence programs, 110

eGym, 111
English Premier League (EPL), 34–35
ESPN, 9, 25, 27, 51
Everesting, xvi
Exercise, 72, 84, 90–91

Federation International de Football (FIFA), 7
  Medical Diploma training program, 2
FIBA International Basketball League, 98–99
2022 FIFA World Cup test, 67
FINA. *See* World Aquatics Federation (FINA)
FitTech of Munich, 84–85
FIVB International Volleyball League, 98
Flash Training, 90–91

Formula 1 international auto racing circuit, 36–37
French Open of Golf, 41–42

German Bundesliga, 8, 16–19
Global Association of International Sport Federations, 45
"Gold Medal Entourage," 66
Golf, xv, xvi, 7, 40–41, 88, 89, 102, 108
Golf Channel, 9

IIHF World Juniors Hockey championship, 64
Indian Premier League's (IPL), 38
International Cycling Union (UCI), 3, 42–43, 88
  with Zwift, 125–127
International Handball Federation, 55–56
International Ice Hockey Federation (IIHF), 6, 51–54
International Olympic Committee, 4, 15–16, 124, 132, 140
International Paralympic Committee, 15–16
International Skating Union (ISU), 54
International Skiing Federation (FIS), 54–55
International Swimming League (ISL), 37–38
International Weightlifting Federation (IWF), 120–121
Investors, 95–99, 111
IRONMAN, 122–124
"IWF Youth World Cup," 120

Kentucky Derby, 57

La Liga, 7, 35, 98, 101
London Marathon, 45–47

Los Angeles Lakers, 26, 27
Los Angeles Marathon, 5
LPGA, 41, 103, 108
"Luca" contact tracing app, 87

Major League Baseball (MLB), 7, 30–32, 101, 104
Major League Soccer (MLS), 27–28, 99
Manchester United football club, 100
Megatlon Fitness Clubs, 89–92
MIT, 76–77
MIT-Sloan Sports Analytics Conference, 44

National Basketball Association (NBA), 6, 25–29, 63, 80, 99, 101–102
National Collegiate Athletic Association (NCAA), 103–104, 122
National Football League (NFL), 32–33, 80, 97–98, 101
National Hockey League (NHL), 29, 63–64, 99
NBC, 135
NCAA's "March Madness" tournament, 7–9, 16, 105, 108
New York Racing Association (NYRA), 57
NHL Ottawa Senators, 80
NYC Half Marathon, 105, 108

Olympic gold medal, 76, 129, 130, 137
Olympic Virtual Series, 124
Olympic records
  COVID-19 pandemic
    athletes with illness, 129–131
    closed loop procedures, 139
    epic challenges, 131–138
    Paris 2024, 141–144
    resilience, 141

Paralympics, 15, 132, 137, 141–143
Paris 2024, 141–144
Peloton, 122–124
PGA Tour, xv

Physical fitness, 65, 72, 84–89
Playbook strategy, 133
Postponements, 9, 14–16, 51–58, 60–61, 106–107, 114
Preakness Stakes, 57
Professional cycling, 42
Professional Golfers Association (PGA), 40–41, 103
Public Health Scotland, 72

Real Madrid football club, 6–7
Rescheduling challenges, 14–15
Restart plan
  English Premier League (EPL), 34–35
  Formula 1 international auto racing circuit, 36–37
  French Open of Golf, 41–42
  Indian Premier League's (IPL), 38
  International Swimming League (ISL), 37–38
  La Liga, 35
  London Marathon, 45–47
  LPGA, 41
  Major League Baseball (MLB), 30–32
  Major League Soccer (MLS), 27–28
  National Football League (NFL), 32–33
  National Hockey League (NHL), 29
  policy decisions, 24–25
  Professional Golfers Association (PGA), 40–41
  Serie A football league, 4, 35–36
  UCI, 42–43
  UFC, 22–24
Rose Bowl Operating Company (RBOC), 114–116
Rubtiler, 110

Serie A football league, 35–36
Silver Lake LLC, 95
Six Nations Rugby, 105
Skate Canada, 121
Sport business
  dynamics of, 110–111
  events, 44–45
  management, xvii–xviii

Sports
  during COVID-19 pandemic
    disruptions, 60–62
    financial losses, xviii, 34, 100
    fitness challenges, 84–89
    issues management, 65–67
    learning experiences, 78–81
    live sports broadcasts, 100–101
    management, 76–77
    prize money payouts, 102–103
    recoveries, 81–84
    resilience, 81–84, 141
    restart plan (*see* Restart plan)
    sports, records, xvi–xvii
    virtual reality, 127
  equipment companies, 108–110
Sports events, 111
  Dubai, 112
  Florida, 112–113
  Mexico, 113
  Switzerland, 113
  United Arab Emirates, 112
Superspreader risk, 10, 58–60
Symbiont, 110

"Taylor Made Driving Relief," 40
Technical University of Berlin, 76, 77
TechnoGym, 89
Test and Trace, 58–60
Texas Medical Association, 77
Tokyo 2020, 16, 136–138
Tokyo Marathon, 1–2, 105
Tokyo 2020 Paralympic Games, 137
Tokyo 2020 Summer Olympics, 79, 131, 132
Top-ranked athletes, xix, xx
Triple Crown, 57

UAE cycling tour, 3
UCI. *See* International Cycling Union (UCI)
UCI 2020 Track Cycling Championships, 3–4
UEFA, 6, 8, 14, 34, 58, 59
UFC, 22–24
"UF Health Screen, Test & Protect," 12
Ultimate Garden Clash, 119
University of Bristol, 72
U.S. Center for Disease Control and Prevention (CDC), 73

Vendee Globe, 39, 40
Virtual Trainer classes, 90

Whoop, xv, 109
Wimbledon 2021, 59
World Aquatics Federation (FINA), 132
World Athletics, 119–120
World Health Organization (WHO), 2–3
World Masters Games 2021, 104
World Rugby, 5, 98

Zero-COVID strategy, 11–12, 49, 108, 113
Zwift, 125–127

OTHER TITLES IN THE SPORTS AND ENTERTAINMENT MANAGEMENT COLLECTION

Lynn Kahle, University of Oregon, Editor

- *Inside the World of a Football Agent* by Gennaro Giulio Tedeschi
- *The Business of Music Management* by Tom Stein
- *The Olympic Sports Economy* by Max Donner
- *Great Coaching and Your Bottom Line* by Marijan Hizak
- *Artist Development Essentials* by Hristo Penchev

Concise and Applied Business Books

The Collection listed above is one of 30 business subject collections that Business Expert Press has grown to make BEP a premiere publisher of print and digital books. Our concise and applied books are for...

- Professionals and Practitioners
- Faculty who adopt our books for courses
- Librarians who know that BEP's Digital Libraries are a unique way to offer students ebooks to download, not restricted with any digital rights management
- Executive Training Course Leaders
- Business Seminar Organizers

Business Expert Press books are for anyone who needs to dig deeper on business ideas, goals, and solutions to everyday problems. Whether one print book, one ebook, or buying a digital library of 110 ebooks, we remain the affordable and smart way to be business smart. For more information, please visit www.businessexpertpress.com, or contact sales@businessexpertpress.com.

CPSIA information can be obtained
at www.ICGtesting.com
Printed in the USA
LVHW060757060623
748933LV00010B/133